HIGH  S

by John E. Meeks, M.D.

Hazelden Educational Materials
Center City, Minnesota 55012-0176

©1988 by Hazelden Foundation
All rights reserved. Published by Hazelden 1994
Originally published by National Medical
Enterprises 1988. Printed in the United States
of America. No portion of this publication may
be reproduced in any manner without the
written permission of the publisher

ISBN: 1-56838-021-6

Editor's note

Hazelden Educational Materials offers a variety of information on chemical dependency and related areas. Our publications do not necessarily represent Hazelden's programs, nor do they officially speak for any Twelve Step organization.

This book is not intended to replace personal medical care and supervision; there is no substitute for the experience and information that your doctor can provide. Rather, it is our hope that this book will provide additional information to help people understand proper use of medication in biopsychiatry.

Proper medical care should always be tailored to the individual patient. If you read something in this book that seems to conflict with your doctor's instructions, contact your doctor. Your doctor may have medically sound reasons for prescribing medication in a manner that may differ from the information presented in this book.

Also note that this book may not contain every drug or brand of drug currently prescribed in the treatment of child and adolescent psychiatric conditions.

If you have questions about any medicine or treatment in this book, consult your doctor or therapist.

In addition, the patient names and cases used in this book do not represent actual people, but are composite cases drawn from several sources.

CONTENTS

*To my parents, John T. and Edna M.
Meeks, who helped me through my own
high times/low times.*

Acknowledgments

I am especially indebted to Karla Dougherty for her invaluable contributions to this book, which benefited greatly from her considerable talents.

I would also like to thank Doctors Laurence Greenwood and Bruce Kehr for their excellent advice and thorough review of the manuscript.

Introduction: The Face in the Mirror

"How can my parents understand me when I don't understand myself?"

—*Cindy, 16*

• Paul idealized his older brother, a star quarterback at school. When Paul became a sophomore, there was no question that he too would try out for the football team. But Paul was built differently from his stocky brother. The coach tried to persuade him to give basketball a shot, but Paul wasn't buying. He *had* to be a football player just like his brother. He didn't make the team and he began to withdraw. . . .

• Susan used to be a vivacious teen, popular and smart. But when she turned sixteen, she began to change. Her schoolwork began to drop. She stopped going out with her friends. She stopped eating. In fact, all Susan wanted to do now was sleep—and scream at her parents to leave her alone. . . .

• Billy was suspended from school—again. Even though he promised his parents that he wouldn't cut any more classes, he didn't say anything about doing the work. In fact, he hadn't handed in an English assignment for six weeks. When the teacher confronted him, Billy was silent for a beat. He then proceeded to throw his books on the floor, kick them, then storm out, shouting, "Who the f—— needs school anyway!"

• Liz hated her looks. When her parents told her that she was pretty, she glared at them. If she was so pretty, why didn't she have any dates? But when she began to wear tight, revealing clothes to school, she noticed that the boys looked at her a lot.

In fact, she began to have more dates than she could handle. Sex became her entry into a different world. Until she became pregnant. . . .

Adolescence. The teenage years. Suddenly your well-behaved youngster has become a sullen monster, your cheerful child a stranger in your own home—unpredictable, defensive, and confused.

Adolescence has become a cliché, a "minority group" of raging hormones and instability. Teenagers are rebellious. They demand impossible attention. They can be rude. They're impatient. "What's the matter with kids today?" is a refrain that has been heard down through the ages since ancient times.

As with any cliché, there is some truth to this one. Just as the elderly, as a group, face certain realities about their bodies, their work, and their view of life, so do adolescents. They are in a time of transition and tremendous growth. They have more energy. They are learning to leave the secure world of childhood with its all-powerful parents to find a place in a complex—and unknown—world.

But accepting the clichéd view of adolescence without looking below the surface can be dangerous. Labeling all teenagers with mood swings as predictable, all adolescents with negative outlooks as typical, and all kids who "act out" excessively as normal can do countless teens a disservice—and cause them real harm.

Many adolescents are not just "going through a stage." They are suffering from depression—and crying out for help.

ADOLESCENTS ARE PEOPLE, TOO

"I hate my parents!"
    "No one understands me."
    "Why doesn't anybody like me?"
    "I don't want to talk about it."
    "Leave me alone!"
As a psychiatrist specializing in the treatment of adolescents for more than twenty-five years—and as a parent of three one-time teenage girls—I have learned to respect the very real pain of growing up and breaking away from one's family. I have

learned to admire the enormous courage and resiliency it takes to find one's role in life. And I have learned to understand—and remember—the problems and issues adolescents face as their everyday realities: achievement in school, acceptance by friends, acclimation to an untested world at large, and more.

Many teens go through this time unscarred. They weather the battle between independence and dependence with little inner turmoil. But others, including those I have treated over the years, become mired in confusion, filled with hopelessness and helplessness, unable to find their way with confidence.

The fact is that despite our best intentions, depression can strike. And it can strike at any age. It is considered the leading mental health problem of our stress-filled times—as well as the major cause of suicide. If depression is so prevalent among adults, why not adolescents? Their body changes, their excess energy, their new and sudden emotions can all translate into a loss of self-esteem, confusion, disillusionment—and depression. Just as with adults, adolescent depression can be a normal—and appropriate—time-limited reaction to a situation. Or it can become a serious problem with a life of its own.

That's why it's so crucial to understand what our teens are going through—and when it's time to intervene.

THE MANY FACES OF ADOLESCENT DEPRESSION

As "typical" as your teen can act at times, you know he or she is not a cliché. Your teenager is unique, and when the bottom falls out, it's easy to feel helpless—and stretched to your limits.

It's difficult for parents to see their child's pain, especially when that inner turmoil is often directed at them. As a parent, you are linked to your child on a primal level; it's almost impossible for you to view your teenager through objective eyes. Further, a confused teenager rarely comes out and asks for help. He or she understands as little of the problem as you.

A crisis needs a solution fast. If your teenager is depressed, you must be able to read the warning signs before depression gets out of hand.

This book is designed to help you read those signs. As it guides you through the complexities of normal adolescent and its sometimes depressive face, it will help you remember what it was like to be young yourself. It offers real understanding and real solutions for depression that can be used not only in the therapist's office but at home.

Depression can be cured. It's hard enough for your teen to go through adolescence without this handicap. I hope that the insights, advice, and examples within these pages will give you the tools you'll need to help your own teenager.

In the first section, you'll discover ways to recognize the different faces of adolescent depression—and which ones need immediate action. In the second section, you will see the destructive ties between today's teens and drugs, learning disabilities, delinquency, and abuse. Finally, in the third section, you will discover how to stop your teen's depression in its tracks: with therapy, with training programs, with medicine, and with a supportive family atmosphere.

A mother of a teenage daughter once told me she saw her role as somewhere between the house clown and an anonymous donor. She was lightly referring to the fact that her teenager didn't take her authority seriously, but cheerfully accepted her financial support. A sense of humor like hers helps. Armed with perspective, we can enjoy our children's teenage years—and appreciate their humorous side. Armed with wisdom, we can offer hope to our young—and their future. Armed with understanding and the right kind of support, we adults can make this journey called adolescence a smoother, more rewarding one— for teenagers and parents alike.

We owe it to our children—and ourselves.

PART I

Through the Looking Glass

CHAPTER ONE

Life as a Teenager

"Children today are tyrants. They contradict their parents, gobble their food, and tyrannize their teachers."

— Socrates (470–399 B.C.)

Think about it: Young Dianus squirming in his seat, preferring to gaze outside at the date trees than listen to his teacher philosophize. Or young Helen, tying and retying her toga in her room while in the corridor her mother is yelling at her in Latin to help with the noonday meal.

I doubt that adolescence in ancient times was quite like these scenarios, but it is a fact that adolescent behavior—and exasperated parents—have been around at least since the days of ancient Egypt, Greece, and Rome. Four thousand years ago, these dire words were carved on a stone tablet in Ur: "Our civilization is doomed if the unheard of actions of our younger generations are allowed to continue."

Maybe Shakespeare had this gloomy prediction in mind when, in *A Winter's Tale*, he wrote, "I would there were no age between ten and three-and-twenty, or that youth would sleep out the rest; for there is nothing in the between but getting wenches with child, wronging the ancientry, stealing, fighting..."

Even during the Dark Ages, there was talk of the transition years. *Le Grand Propriétaire*, written in 1556, mentions "the third age, which is called adolescence... ends in the twenty-first year... and it can go on till thirty or thirty-five. This age is called adolescence because the person is big enough to beget children. In this age the limbs are soft and able to grow and receive strength and vigor from natural heat."

Since teens in medieval days were often married by the time

they reached puberty, their adolescence, in reality, was short-lived. Considered "little adults," teenagers were expected to pull their weight at an early age. We can only imagine the inner turmoil silently faced by a young girl about to meet her equally young husband for the first time on her wedding night. Or a young boy, restless and curious, forced to spend the long daylight hours in the fields, bending and lifting and toiling day after day.

The fact is that adolescent turmoil has been around as long as there have been teenagers. Yes, today adolescents live under the cloud of nuclear war. Yes, they are bombarded by facts and fantasies in magazines, television, and on film. Yes, more often than not, they have been raised in households where both mothers and fathers work, where day care and live-in help have filled the gaps of parenting. But is this any harder than being raised in households at the turn of the century, when fathers maintained exact and total control? When rules were rigid and unabiding? When death from disease could strike at any time?

Life has always been difficult for our youth. It's *how* it's difficult that changes over time. The stress has always been there—whether it was the Great Depression, a World War, or even a polio epidemic. Listen:

In America, between 1790 and 1840, kids who had been reared on farms suddenly had to adjust to city life as families began the migration from rural to urban locales. No longer was it a *fait accompli* to become a farmer. Teenagers could become lawyers, clerks, shopkeepers... the choices were as limitless—and as confusing—as they are today.

But more social turmoil was in the wind. With the advent of the Industrial Revolution in 1880, there were radical changes in lower- and middle-class households. The poor could suddenly become rich. Parents, working almost around the clock, no longer had the time or the patience to pay much attention to their kids. And the kids themselves were put to work on factory lines at an early age, becoming old before their time. Social, economic, and political changes occurred as fast and as furiously as today....

Whether or not life is harder today really doesn't matter. The important point to remember is that *now* is all the adolescent has. History rarely helps.

WHAT'S THE MATTER WITH PARENTS TODAY?

It's been more years than I care to count since I've been a teenager. But I still remember, as if it were yesterday, the time my eighth-grade math teacher told me, "You looked good on the football field the other day."

Wow! A compliment from an adult! I kept hearing her remark every afternoon I showed up for practice. It was all coming together: the roar of the crowd . . . the applause . . . the admiration of the girls and the other guys. Everything was sure to go my way—except that in an early game I fumbled the ball and the other team got the touchdown. Then I *really* needed to remember the teacher's compliment.

Adolescence is an impressionable age. Its rites and its achievements stick with us all our lives. Think back to your teenage years. The way you felt when a teacher smiled and said, "Good work." Or the first time you and your date dressed up and did the town. Or that first afternoon you legally drove the family car. Or the thrill when your date first let you hold hands or—ecstasy!—kiss.

Unfortunately, the rejections of adolescence remain with us as well. The fight you had with your best friend. The failure during cheerleader tryouts. The phone call where the girl or boy you loved passionately said goodbye. We might not remember the actual situations, but we can still remember the way we felt. No matter how old we are, we all still have some memory of that adolescent intensity.

But teenagers experience these peaks and valleys on a daily basis. And it's important for us, as parents, to try to remember what that was like. Only then can we understand that these situations have the same impact on our youth as our adult day-to-day stresses—without maturity and perspective to help cushion the blows.

Our views of adolescence are not only clouded by the passage of time. We also can harbor unconscious and irrational attitudes toward our own children. We may feel competitive, fearful, envious, and even erotic toward our adolescents—without ever being fully conscious of these conflicting emotions. We may also see ourselves (or think that we do) in our children. This can lead to excessive criticism of our faults that we believe they exhibit (or that we think we see in them) or unrealistically high expectations when they carry our "flawed genius."

Further, many parents have their own preconceived expectations and notions about teenagers and how they should be raised. We give adolescents minority group status, treating them as a group, a subculture, instead of individual people. This is perpetuated by the fact that teenagers do tend to cluster together, whether it be at school or at a social event.

And, as individuals, they must cope with a vastly different world than the one in which we grew up, a new world where geographical mobility, corporate politics, illegal drugs, economics, global influence, and AIDS all condition and mold their development. And that's not even mentioning TV or cinematic sex and violence. What worked for us might not work for them. A child who, on the surface, seems to be too "laid back" and easily swayed might actually be coping better with the world of the eighties than one whose principles and beliefs never budge.

As parents, we must look at the bigger picture, both in ourselves and in our kids. Before we make judgments, however, we must have all the facts.

TYPICAL TEENS

To understand why teenagers get depressed, you have to first understand why teenagers act the way they do. Here, then, are the whys of adolescence:

"Flying the Coop"
Stacey had a loving relationship with her parents. Ever since she could remember, Mom and Dad were there, hugging her, telling her how much they loved her, and stopping her tears. She depended on them for everything, from food on the table to summer vacations. But when she turned twelve, she began to shy away from their love. When her mother made roast beef for

dinner, Stacey would tell her she hated meat. When her father gave her a hug, Stacey would squirm away. The glowing, receptive child had turned into a teenager. . . .

When children are small, their entire universe is their parents. Their sense of safety, self-esteem, and stability all stem from the love and warmth they receive from Mom and Dad. But as they approach adolescence, they start to feel embarrassed about their dependency on their parents. Suddenly, it feels babyish to care so much about them. Only little kids let their parents tell them what to do and how to behave. To be grown up means to be independent.

Suddenly that parental well of self-esteem is dry—without any inner confidence to fill it back up. Since teenagers have yet to experience the self-confidence that comes from "flying solo," they are constantly pulled between wanting independence from their parents and the need to be dependent on them. "Why do I always have to throw out the garbage!" they'll say one minute— but the next, they'll be complaining that you never listen to what they have to say.

One of the ways teenagers deal with this "push-pull" is to develop "straw men"—a term coined by psychologist Erik Erikson.

Their internal superego, or conscience, is the representative of the adored and powerful parent of early childhood. It is a fearful obstacle to growth. But if they externalize this superego by knocking their parents—the straw men—off their pedestal, they can have an easier time pulling away. For example, say your son is sitting in the backseat of the car. The highway is clear and, as you usually do, you're going an easy ten miles over the speed limit. Suddenly your son pipes up. "Dad, aren't you going over the limit? Isn't that against the law? You always told me to obey the law. Guess that makes you a criminal."

It's not easy for parents who were once considered gods, basking in godlike attention, to get knocked down, but it's a normal part of growing up.

"A Friend in Need"
Bob is not a baby. He hasn't been since he was thirteen—as he has told his parents countless times. But inside, he's going through that push and pull of independence versus depen-

dence. He doesn't have his parents any more to shower him with self-esteem, but he hasn't been out in the world enough to have the confidence that comes from within. He knows he feels great when he's hanging around with his friends. He feels confident and secure and accepted. So why not see them after school for a couple of hours? And on Saturday nights? And, when he's at home with his parents—who, in his mind, continue to treat him like a baby—why not give his friends a call? Soon Bob is spending most of his waking hours with the guys.

When teenagers feel this unconscious vacuum of low self-esteem, they need it filled fast. Friends fit the bill perfectly. If they can be friends with kids they consider cool or popular, then they can feel cool, too. These relationships are usually narcissistic and superficial. They fulfill a need, they repair some ego damage, but they are no deeper than a pool's reflection. Because they are a "quick fix," young teenagers will constantly be wondering if this group is the *right* group. Are they really the most popular? Is she really as cool a dresser as I think she is? What if he's really a nerd? Relationships end as fast as they begin. Friends are dropped. Rejections ripple through the group.

There is no doubt that to kids there is safety in numbers. Teenage cliques, complete with fads, language, and dress styles, form a counterculture, a solid front to show—at least on the surface—their superiority over adults who are too old-fashioned even to know what is cool.

When teenagers mature and begin to develop a genuine self-image, they become more comfortable with themselves. They no longer need friends for a "fix." Instead, they start making *real* friends—people they like for who they are, not what they seem to be or are "seen to be." And they'll be prepared to defend that friendship to anyone who questions it. "I don't think Joe's a jerk. He's really a great person. Maybe he's a little quiet, but he's okay."

"Rock Around the Clock"

Ellen's mother was amazed. She watched her daughter come in at eleven at night, get up at the crack of dawn the next morning, jog around the block, then spend the day at the beach with her friends. Ellen was always moving. She'd dance while she washed the dishes; she'd drum her pencil and kick her legs when she sat at her desk doing homework. The girl never stopped!

It's a fact: Adolescents are active, more active than they will ever be again. Biologically, there's that spurt of hormones surging through their body, especially testosterone, estrogen, adrenaline, and steroids—hormones that translate chemically into high activity.

Teenagers also experience an increase in voluntary muscle mass. Famed child psychologist Jean Piaget found that once children learn something, they will repeat it over and over again until they master it. This recently developed muscle mass is new and it must be used—over and over again. . . .

There are psychological reasons, too, why adolescents are so active. Passivity implies that dreaded dependence, while activity means independence. Further, it's around this time that kids are supposed to be doing things. People rarely ask teenagers how they feel or what they think. Rather, it's "What are you going to do? What do you want to be?" Instead of "What do you think of girls?" a teenage boy is asked, "Do you have a girlfriend?"

Finally, activity comes from society itself. Suddenly a teenager is allowed to do more than ever before. She can take the family car for a ride. He can stay out later. She can buy her own shampoo. You no longer have to hold his hand when he crosses the street.

Your kids are busy with their own lives. They are actively growing up.

"Whistling in the Dark"

His mother would call it a swagger, but Sam liked to walk around with his head held high, his gait sure and confident. The problem was that it was all a facade. He might have looked like a big shot, but inside he was terrified.

Kids like to take on roles. They are beginning to believe in their abilities, but their talents don't yet match their expectations. They see what they need to do to "make it" in the world, but they haven't yet been tested. Because deep down they're scared to death, they'll exaggerate their confidence, rattling off their grandiose schemes and exhibiting a bravado they don't feel.

Like the boy who wanted to be the football player his brother was, teenagers get notions about what would raise their self-esteem and, come hell or high water, they're gonna do it—even if it isn't right for them.

Another example: Let's say the "coolest" shoes to wear to school this year are slip-on heels. A teenage girl goes into the shop to buy a pair—but they don't have her size. She'll buy a size smaller, knowing they'll be much too tight, because she has to have them to feel accepted.

"I Love You/I Hate You"
It was enough to drive a mother crazy. One day Martha would be high as a kite, chattering away, feeling ten feet tall. The next day (or even that same night), she'd be crying into her pillow, hating the world and everything in it.

There's no doubt about it: Teenagers' moods are erratic. Part of it stems from the push and pull between wanting to depend on their parents and pushing them away. In their minds, it's their parents who swing back and forth. One day, Martha's mother is beaming over her report card. The next day, she's screaming because Martha's clothes are strewn all over the floor.

The world of teenagers is an unstable place. Not only are many of their "trendy" early friendships rocky, but year after year, their reality keeps changing. Think about it. Let's say you are a teenager, doing great in school and feeling pretty smart. But the school year ends. Next year is completely different. New teachers, new subjects, new classmates. Suddenly, you're "stupid" all over again!

Teenagers haven't yet learned to live with ambivalence. They don't yet know their strengths and their weaknesses. That will only come with time.

"Me, Myself, and I"
All John could think about was himself. Like the actress who talked about her career all night over dinner, only to say, "Enough about me. What did you think of my play?" it was me, me, me, day and night.

John was not alone. Adolescence is a very self-centered time. As we have seen, teenagers form early friendships to enhance themselves. They have to restore a sense of themselves. This need is so great that they can't possibly have room for other people and their problems. Further, they will ignore any characteristics that do not correspond with their needs or their views of the world. A colleague of mine was treating a fourteen-year-old boy for several weeks. During each of their sessions, the therapist always wore his wedding ring. After some time had passed, the boy looked at him with surprise. "I didn't know you were married. I thought you were the bachelor type." Ironically, several of his other adolescent patients saw him as an "old-fashioned square" from the start.

The adolescent is in the eye of the storm. Hormones within . . . demands swirling outside . . . the teenager holds himself together by focusing on getting his needs met. This self-centered attitude reduces his dependency on his parents while asserting his separateness from them, since his needs are different from theirs.

"Master of the Universe"

Ruth's family used to enjoy peaceful dinners. The conversation would ebb and flow between some gossip, some questions about school, and please pass the potatoes. But lately Ruth has been monopolizing the table. All she does is talk, talk, talk—about ideas, about changing the world, about philosophy. . . .

Adolescents are exercising their brains. Before puberty, they had learned to manipulate isolated problems and to come to intellectual conclusions logically. Now, however, their brains can decipher and conceptualize the relationships between different thoughts, different facts, and different possibilities. In the same way that they exercise their new voluntary muscle mass, teenagers repeat their new ability to think abstractly over and over again until they master it. They also try to use this new strength to intellectually "out-muscle" their parents, again reinforcing the move to independence.

This new intellectual capability subdues with time, never to be so intense again. It is why the greatest composers and mathematicians have often done their best work in their late adolescence and young adult years.

"Born to Be Wild"
Tim has already seen *The Wild One* a few dozen times. He rolls up his T-shirts, sweeps back his hair, and dreams of owning a motorcyle someday. When he's not listening to Bruce Springsteen at full volume in his room, he's out with his friends, hanging out at the local diner.

Some teenagers will act out. Not only does rebelliousness translate into freedom, but keeping busy keeps the demons of fear and uncertainty away. "I'm bored" is not simply a spoiled teen's lament. It is an anxious voice trying to stay one step ahead of fear.

EXPRESSIVE FACES

In the 1970s a male rock singer named Alice Cooper skyrocketed up the charts. His shtick? He played his "heavy metal" music accompanied by snakes, white make-up, elaborate sets, and colored smoke. As a grand finale, he'd blow up his guitar. Art, no. Expensive, yes. But young teenagers everywhere were willing to pay to see his combination guerrilla theater, hard rock, and special effects mirror their fantasies and confusion—at least until other groups jumped on the "rock as theater" bandwagon.

Activity also diverts attention. If a teenager is busy acting belligerent and angry, he or she can hide a less acceptable emotion. A boy yelling at his parents could be disguising his gentler, "babyish" love for them.

Occasionally, teenagers will stop running to stand up and face the inner enemy. But they won't do it alone. They need a listener—and that usually means you. They will talk and talk about their problems, soothing their fears with words, until the demons—or you—fall asleep.

"Walk on a Crack/Break Your Mother's Back"
Susan gobbled up horror novels like candy. She loved anything occult, and she always read her horoscope in the morning. The supernatural was her constant companion, and, to her parent's consternation, she was always reading everything as a good or bad omen.

Many teenagers love the occult. To them, it's not a frightening unknown—it's pure entertainment. They visit haunted houses. They go to get their fortunes read. It is a demon they can identify, an unknown they can play with and come away intact.

Teenagers are human beings, individuals at an age where changes—from voices to emotions—come fast and furiously. They know that a lot of new things will be expected of them very soon, and they don't have a clue as to whether they'll be able to do them . . . or if they'll be good at them.

In spite of their tenuous position, many teenagers come through adolescence with no turmoil at all. In fact, a series of groundbreaking studies by Dr. Daniel Offer over the last decade proved that the majority of teens have lives that would make Beaver Cleaver jealous. Their adolescence is fulfilling, happy, and enjoyable. Dr. Offer found that most teenagers:

- Do not feel inferior and do not feel that others treat them badly
- Are relaxed
- Can control themselves in most situations
- Are proud of their body's development
- Believe they are strong and healthy
- Do not wish to be supported for the rest of their lives
- Are not afraid of sexual feelings
- Make friends easily
- Have no problems with their parents
- Are optimistic and hopeful about their future

But Dr. Offer also discovered that 20 percent of all adolescents *do* suffer. They see life as empty, an endless problem with no answers in sight. Of these 3.4 million teens, only 1.7 million receive treatment.

These are the millions of adolescents who suffer from depression. But even if there was only one depressed teen, it would be one too many if it is your child who is hurting.

Before I discuss adolescent depression in greater detail, take a moment to take the following quiz. It will help you recognize if your child is going through the normal changes of adolescence or if he or she is depressed and in need of help.

IS YOUR TEENAGER DEPRESSED?

These statements are divided into three sections: school, home, and outside activities. Each one describes a potential situation where depression can set in or symptoms of depression are already in place. Think them over. See if any apply to you and your family. Mark those statements you feel are true about your teenager, whether they concern something you have observed directly or learned indirectly—from a teacher, a doctor, or someone in your community.

Your Teenager at School
1. My son has been sleeping late in the mornings and I can't seem to get him up to go to school.
2. My daughter's grades have been slipping.
3. My son is spending more time on his homework—and less and less time with his friends.
4. Last night my daughter cried herself to sleep because she didn't get an A on an exam.
5. My son's been cutting classes.
6. My daughter's I.Q. is exceptional, but she keeps failing in school.
7. My son was too sick to go to school—again.
8. My daughter wants to drop out of college.
9. My son never studies.
10. My daughter's been complaining about her teachers this year, but they don't seem too bad to me.
11. Graduation is coming up.
12. My son got rejected from the college of his choice.
13. My son was passed up for the basketball team.
14. My daughter makes straight As, but she's always terrified she will flunk her tests.

Your Teenager at Home
15. My son spends all his time away from home.
16. My daughter sits in her room with the door closed night after night.

17. The phone never rings for my son.
18. My daughter would prefer to hang around with our friends that be with kids her own age.
19. My son always has friends over to the house but never the same ones twice.
20. Both of us work, and we never seem to have enough time together as a family.
21. We're separated. The kids seem in shock about it.
22. I'm a widow.
23. My son is fascinated by death.
24. My daughter won't talk to me.
25. My son looks up to his older brother and wants to be just like him.
26. My daughter's room is a terrible mess.
27. My son doesn't shower.
28. My daughter hasn't been eating.
29. My son has his light on all night long.
30. My daughter's been having terrible nightmares.
31. My son is very moody. He gets down for no reason.
32. My daughter sits in her room and plays the same sad song over and over.
33. My daughter isn't as popular as her sister.
34. Lately my son starts screaming at me for no reason.
35. Last night my son broke a window because he was having a tantrum.
36. My son just lost a close relative (grandfather, uncle, etc.).
37. My daughter has a "don't care" attitude.
38. My son sits and listens to music on his headphones hour after hour every night.
39. My daughter jokes about suicide.
40. Our divorce just became final.

Your Teenager and Outside Activities
41. My husband is a heavy drinker—sometimes an abusive one.
42. My son is always getting speeding tickets.
43. My daughter is on five committees, three councils, and she is in an advanced class at school. She seems to be handling it all, but I don't know how she does it.
44. My son has a rigid exercise schedule.

45. My daughter is dressing much too provocatively, but when I tell her to change, she starts to scream at me.
46. We just moved to a new home and the kids don't like the neighborhood.
47. My son's friend was killed in an auto accident.
48. I think my daughter's pregnant.
49. My son is just recovering from a bout of mono.
50. My daughter's leg has been in a cast all winter.
51. A boy in school committed suicide.
52. My daughter doesn't see her friends any more.
53. My son's girlfriend broke up with him last night.
54. My daughter has had a series of car wrecks lately.
55. My daughter has dropped all of her hobbies.

If *several* of these statements ring true to you, it is possible that your teenager may be suffering from depression—either a normal grief reaction all of us feel at one time or another, a more serious reactive depression, a deeply rooted chronic depression, or a major affective disorder. But remember: these statements are generalizations only. If you feel your teen is in the throes of adolescent depression, you should speak to your physician—and to your child. And you should continue reading . . . .

CHAPTER TWO:

What Is Depression?

"Even a thought, even a possibility, can shatter us and transform us."

—*Nietzsche*

From the moment Allison entered my office, I knew she was depressed. Her hair was unkempt, her clothes thrown together. She wouldn't look at me; she stared at the floor, sullen and withdrawn.

Allison's parents wanted her to see me. She was going to drop out of college in her freshman year because she hated it. She saw no reason to go to school. Her parents were at their wit's end.

What made it so difficult for Allison and her parents was that prior to going off to school, she had been bright, enthusiastic, and hopeful about her future. She had planned to study law.

Allison had prided herself as being a girl who could handle any problem life threw at her. If homework seemed overwhelming, she plunged in and did it anyway. If a friend was upset, it was Allison who got the phone call. She always had the right thing to say. Even her relationship with her parents was good. They offered her guidance, praised her when she handled something well, and they respected her privacy.

All in all, Allison had seemed to be a normal, well-adjusted teen—until her boyfriend broke up with her. Suddenly, she had no control. She couldn't make him care for her again, no matter what she did. Instead of getting angry, Allison blamed herself. The breakup was all her fault. Ashamed and guilt-ridden, she was too terrified to talk about it. She was afraid she'd be rejected again. Instead, Allison made a monumental effort to put on a brave face, going through the motions at school, at extracurricular activities, and at home.

But driving up to college proved to be too much. Allison was frozen. She was terrified of this strange new world where no one would understand her, where no one could possibly love her. She pretended all was well, but when her parents drove off, she burst into tears.

It was this scared, frightened side of Allison that her new roommates met. They couldn't penetrate what they perceived as Allison's self-pity. After a while, they didn't even try. Soon Allison became her own self-fulfilling prophecy: unloved, unnoticed, and out of control.

Though it appeared that Allison's depression stemmed from her boyfriend's rejection, in reality, it had begun long before. Allison's depression and low self-esteem had always been there, lying just below the surface, ready to erupt at the first provocation. Through therapy, she began to realize how she had been living a life that others wanted for her rather than one of her own. She saw that she frequently hid her real emotions for fear of losing the love and security she received for being "good."

Happily, Allison's depression began to lift after only two weeks on an antidepressant. Armed with the knowledge and strength she gained in a brief series of therapy sessions, Allison transferred to a different school, and today she's an outspoken associate in a growing law firm.

But this story might have had a different ending if Allison had not come in for treatment. At the time, she was a teenager in pain, suffering from depression—but she could have walked into my office with the same problem ten, twenty, even thirty years later. The fact is that depression knows no age or time. It can strike anyone, teenager and adult alike.

Before we go on to the specific signs and symptoms of adolescent depression, I'd like to spend a few pages on depression itself—what it is and what it is not:

MYTH # 1: Depression is all in the mind, or, the "Come on, cheer up!" theory.

Wrong. Depression is a disease, with as much a biological component as tuberculosis, arteriosclerosis, or the common cold. It appears when the brain's chemical "messengers" malfunction, interrupting the normal passage of information from brain cell to brain cell.

These physical changes have been demonstrated through a variety of tests:

The EEG (Electroencephalograph).

This test measures the electrical response of the brain when a patient is subjected to a stimulus change, such as a flash of light or a loud noise. Depressed people show very little electrical "surge" in their brains. Their electrical impulses stay unaroused. This finding is a sign that the brain is not processing information normally. On a daily basis it shows up as confusion, faulty memory, and difficult thinking in depressed patients.

The DST (Dexamethasone Suppression Test).

This is one of several neuroendocrine tests, concentrating on hormonal secretions in the brain instead of electric impulses. Here, a patient gets an injection of the chemical dexamethasone which in nondepressed people suppresses the hormone called cortisol. But if a patient is suffering from depression, the cortisol level stays the same.

It's important to remember that the findings of these tests are not "etched in stone." A hospital study of 33 depressed and 51 nondepressed teens by Dr. Aman U. Khan found that only 69.9 percent of the depressed teens had positive DST results and only 82 percent of the nondepressed group had negative results. There are many situations that will give a false positive result, even though a person is not depressed. Conditions such as pregnancy, diabetes, alcohol withdrawal, and severe weight loss can all keep cortisol at its high level during a DST diagnosis. But, when combined with an accurate family and personal history, tests such as the DST can be considered proof positive.

The good news is that these physical changes are not permanent. They disappear when depression is successfully treated.

MYTH # 2: All a depressed person needs is someone to listen, or, the "They only want sympathy" theory.

It is helpful to have a sympathetic listener, but not always. Because many depressions have a biological base, various medications may be needed to counteract their impact. Called antidepressants, these pills help correct the chemical imbalance in the brain. Supervised and regulated by your doctor, an effective dosage can alleviate depression's more severe symptoms. Medications such as MAO inhibitors block the action of monamine oxidase, an enzyme which, when malfunctioning, breaks down the brain's neurotransmitters and causes depression. Tricylic antidepressants (TCAs) such as Elavil increase the chemical neurotransmitters in the brain via a different route that, in many cases, works more effectively. TCAs also have fewer side effects and are usually safer to use than MAO inhibitors. Lithium helps restore a balance between high and low moods and may prevent depression in some patients.

But pills alone cannot cure depression. Psychotherapy, medicine, family support, and skill training all play a role, and these will be discussed in detail in Part III.

MYTH # 3: Depressed people are always withdrawn and quiet, or, the "You can tell by looking at them" theory.

Not true. Depressed adolescents can seem highly agitated, irritable, and uncooperative. They may be viewed as angry troublemakers, but inwardly, they can be very depressed—even suicidal.

MYTH # 4: Depression is inherited, or, the "Cast your fate to the wind" theory.

There is some truth to this one, because family history can help in making an accurate diagnosis of depression. But many people who have depression in their family never get it themselves—

and vice versa. Stress can set off depression, as can a traumatic life event. Even a physical ailment can bring on depression.

But facts are facts, and the biological past may be passed along to the present. The individual with a family history may be more vulnerable to depression. In fact, some kinds of depression (e.g., manic depressive disorders) rarely seem to occur without a family history of the disease.

MYTH # 5: Women suffer from depression more than men, or, the "feminine mystique" theory.

This is a complicated statement. Some researchers think so, but others don't. In any case, women reach out for help faster than men, which is why statistics strongly support this myth. Women's symptoms are also often less extreme. However, women often go through daily routines without visible signs of pain; they are better able to disguise depression.

MYTH # 6: Depression is a modern disease, a symptom of the eighties, or, the "It's only a fad" theory.

Yes, depression is a byproduct of our complex lives. Every ten years it has been observed to be on the increase, and, today there are an estimated one hundred million depressed people in the world. *But*—depression has been around since the days of ancient Egypt. It has been called melancholia, madness, the vapors, possession and frailty. Throughout history, people have taken to their beds or the bottle, fainted on the spot, and stayed behind closed doors without ever knowing that the root of their pain was depression.

FAMOUS FACES

Famed writer Graham Greene called his adolescent depression "boredom"—a trait he inherited from his mother, who found motherhood so boring that she had no baby books and no maternal inclinations. Greene followed suit, deciding that life was so boring that it wasn't worth much. He took up Russian roulette for real. Lo and behold, his boredom vanished every time he pulled the trigger. For one and a half years, he had his Russian roulette "fix," until, through psychoanalysis and literary accomplishment, his life no longer seemed so drab.

MYTH # 7: A depressed person is easy to recognize, or, the "You can judge a book by its cover" theory.

This can be true sometimes, especially when a person is withdrawn and quiet. But depression can also be masked. A woman who feels tired all the time could really be in the throes of depression. A man suffering from chest pains could be having an anxiety attack. That's why it's crucial for doctors to do a "differential diagnosis" to determine exactly what is wrong with a patient. Depressed adolescents also have their own kinds of disguises, which are discussed later on.

Depression is insidious, but the myths surrounding it make things even worse. Unfortunately, beliefs are difficult to destroy. Despite the inroads we have made in medicine, in our attitudes, and in our world, people still attach a stigma to this disease. Even in today's sophisticated world, depression is still considered failure, a fatal flaw that must be hidden from others at all costs.

Depression must come out of its closet. It must be examined, understood, and helped—especially when it comes to our teenagers.

Let's go on to that examination, to see how and why adolescents get depressed. It's only a short jump from there to understanding, help . . . and hope.

CHAPTER THREE
Why Kids Get Depressed

"Why can't I love anyone? Why can't I care about myself? Why can't I keep friends? Why do I hurt people all the time? Why can't I be straight? I can't think of any solutions ... all I can think about is the questions and problems that face me."

—*Marti, 15*

We might all feel like kids at heart, but in official terms, adolescence begins with puberty (around twelve for girls; around thirteen and a half for boys) and ends when financial independence—often combined with marriage—is achieved. Today, many teenagers graduate high school, marry, and get jobs, making them certified adults by eighteen. But countless others go on to college and graduate school, continuing to need their family's financial support along the way. For these teens, adolescence can continue—possibly to a parent's chagrin—until twenty-eight or twenty-nine years of age. Adolescent depression—with its unique causes and its need for specific treatment—can strike anywhere along this time frame.

Psychologist Jean Piaget compared a teenager to a philosopher, a person "who ponders his place in the world and struggles with his attempts to make sense of life." Some teens embrace this struggle with vigor and little turmoil. Others find the passage from childhood to the adult world fraught with confusion. As we have discovered in the previous chapters, it almost seems that the question is not why some teens get depressed, but why most teens never do.

Basically, it's the luck of the draw. I have seen mothers and fathers who have demonstrated both their love and their abilities to let go shake their heads in despair over their drug-addicted teens. I have seen very caring parents have children who become depressed, mired in hopelessness and despair. But I have also seen distracted, inattentive parents raise teenagers who never have any problems in their adolescent years.

On the other hand, I have seen depressed parents pass on their pain to their kids.

The fact is that growing up is very complicated. There are no rigid guidelines as to why some kids come out of adolescence unscathed while others are filled with pain. However, there are specific pitfalls, certain signposts up ahead, that signal depression's traps:

The push and pull of independence versus dependency.

When kids turn away from their parents—their nourishing source of self-esteem—many are left with a nagging, empty feeling that doesn't go away.

The fragility of teenage friendships.

When kids start connecting with what they hope are the "right" group of friends, there's a very real chance of rejection. The self-oriented, insecure character of these teenage friendships almost guarantees that, at one point or another, a child will get hurt.

The fluctuating mood swings that are part and parcel of a teenager's life.

As we have seen, ambivalence is not yet a way of life for a teen. Learning to live with shades of gray comes only with maturity. In the meantime, teens fly high from daily achievements, then spiral down when they fail. A teenager can get trapped on one of those mood swings and plummet into despair.

The enormous physical, emotional, and mental changes that sweep through a teenager's mind and body.

Like warriors in battle behind enemy lines, teenagers are continually attacked by change—a multipronged assault that aims for their self-esteem. Their uneven, unpredictable body changes, their surge of sexual and (in their minds) forbidden impulses, their need to knock their parents off their pedestal, chipping away at that valuable source of nourishment—all of these add fuel to depression. In many teens, they create a sense of deep inner loss.

As Erik Erikson discovered, kids do not ask "Who am I?" but "What do I want to make of myself and what do I have to work with?" This complex, weighty question can lead many teens down the road to depression.

ALL THE WORLD'S A STAGE

Think of teenagers as actors in search of the part that will put them over the top. Sometimes they see a stage filled with bad amateurs, ready to be astounded and molded by them. Other times, they suffer from stage fright, seeing themselves with so little talent that they can't even try out for a walk-on part.

Teenagers will—and should—try on many different roles. They savor them all, validate them, and sometimes excessively wear them out in order to hang on to something, anything, that will give them a base of security.

Normal adolescents rehearse their new lines, but they have another play waiting in the wings just in case this particular part doesn't work out. Depressed adolescents, on the other hand, feel the weight of only that one part. Like actors typecast in the same roles forever, they never feel they can try—or be—anything else. They paint themselves into a corner where even the fire exits are closed.

Sometimes depressed adolescents remake *Rebel Without a Cause*, acting out their fear in delinquency, anger, and rebellion. But other depressed teens never give a clue to their fear. They wear their actor's mask for every confining, hopeless performance.

In fact, the turmoil endured by depressed adolescents is, more times than not, a purely internal one. Most teenagers are not rebels. They are young "organization" men and women, who dress, talk, and think alike, ready to follow the first leader they can find. The *real* rebellion is inside. It is a fight against the memories of their old parental attachments. It is a battle against the fear that their ideas of life and their roles in the world at large will come up short. It is a war that can lead to depression—and worse.

FALSE FACES

MYTH: The generation gap is bigger than ever.

FACT: Margaret Mead made this phrase popular during the 1960s, when she concluded that adults were strangers in a strange land when it came to teenage fashion, values, behavior, and language. But whether the '60s, '70s, or the '80s, the truth is that children are remarkably like their parents. Studies done by Dr. Daniel Yankelovich in 1974 and Dr. Daniel Offer in 1970 proved that whether it be religion, politics, social standing, values, career expectations, or economic goals, teenagers and their parents frequently see eye to eye. The hippies of the sixties are now the married parents of two living in the suburbs. The "Me Generation" adolescents of the seventies are today protesting nuclear arms and feeding the homeless. Adults like to think of teenagers as the future's hope. If they believe that kids are different, that they can galvanize society and solve our problems, the world has a chance to be a better place. But in reality, kids could never change the world: They are not equipped with enough knowledge or experience in adolescence to make an effective difference.

WHEN DEPRESSION IS NORMAL...

Teenagers get depressed. Period. Their instability, their vulnerability, their fluctuating moods—all signal times when depression might strike. But as adolescents continue to grow, so does their self-esteem. They begin to find a place in the world, and they are better equipped to steer a steadier course. No longer do their emotions run rampant.

If your child's depression only lasts a week or two, there's no cause for alarm. It's natural to hurt when we suffer a loss, and teenagers are no exception. Whether it is the death of someone close, a divorce, a geographical move, or a rejection, loss hurts.

And healing takes time. During a normal grieving process, teenagers act more passive and dependent, turning into children who need tender loving care. They mourn. They get angry. They act out. And they eventually accept their loss. Slowly, over time, they start going out into the world again, donning their independence and moving forward.

...AND WHEN IT ISN'T

Sometimes depression has a momentum of its own. Sometimes what starts out as a normal response to loss ends up a way of life. Deeply depressed teens stay passive; they never move beyond their pain. Their response to an external loss turns inward, becoming a monster of self-hate. Though at times, they seem to have a brighter disposition, it is merely a reprieve. One scratch, one minor trauma, and they plummet into the depths of despair again.

Depressed teens continue to have problems with human relationships. They might reject support or they might *demand* it—but in such an annoying, selfish way that they never get it.

THE STORIES BEHIND THE FACES

Sometimes one picture can hold a thousand words. In the next few pages, I'll present "word pictures" of the different "types" of adolescents who get depressed. Remember, these are proto-types, not individuals, but they may give you some clues to your own teenagers' makeup and maybe their vulnerability to depression.

1. "Type A" Kids.
"I've got to have that A+. I know that's stupid, but that's what I have to do!"

That's Jaynie talking, a Type A teenage girl. She's a tall, bright, and charismatic fourteen-year-old who moved to an Eastern metropolitan area from Texas. Jaynie's parents are both successful, but they never tried to push her. She has a younger sister who is as easygoing as Jaynie is intense.

Before Jaynie came East, she enjoyed a more laid-back lifestyle. She had had a close group of serious friends, but their earnestness was tempered by athletics. After long, serious conversations, they'd jump on horses and ride.

But in her new high school, competition was the name of the

game. Most of the other teenagers handled it fine; they were able to laugh off the competitive edge. But Jaynie got hooked. It stirred her up. She entered the competition with relish—she *had* to win.

In addition to this competitive drive, Jaynie missed her friends and was angry at her father for making the family move away. But Jaynie, like all Type A kids, prided herself on her intellect. Logically, she knew her father had to move, that he was going toward a better job. She couldn't verbalize her anger—only her shame and guilt that she could be so illogical, so "stupid" as to be angry with him.

Added to this mix was the fact that Jaynie felt her emotions were betraying her, that she was so weak that she had to come in and talk to a "damn shrink!"

Jaynie is not alone. All Type A teenagers are driven to succeed. They pride themselves on their ability to handle things. They fear dependency with a passion. And when they fall, they fall hard.

Consider a Type A adult: the man or woman who is driven to excel, who never seems to stop. Vivacious, charming, brilliant, and energetic, Type As seem too good to be true. These superboys and supergirls are the same way—only years younger and without experience in the world.

Below their surface confidence, Type A kids suffer from low self-esteem. Their way to build themselves up comes from outside achievements. The better they do in school, the better people they will seem. The more friends they have, the more they can validate their success. The more success they find, the better they will feel.

Because these kids are so bright and so energetic, they do succeed for a time—and feel on top of the world. But inside, their anxiety is building. They know their position is precarious, that perfection is impossible to attain. They get depressed when they don't win—and by the fact that they know they won't always win. One minor problem—a B instead of an A, an insensitive comment, a fight with a friend—and the Type A teenager can slide into severe depression. That's why a Type A kid suffers tremendous anxiety before an exam—from hand sweats to compulsive late-night studying.

Unfortunately, many adults don't realize that these superboys and supergirls feel as dependent as other teens. They too need support, but they don't always get it. Pushed into an "all or nothing" corner, the only choice some Type A kids see is suicide. As Charlie Brown of *Peanuts* fame once said, "It's a great burden to be a young person of promise."

2. The Nay-Sayers

Some teenagers are the opposite of the Type A personality. Success seems so out of reach that they don't even try. These teens live in a drab, hopeless world where losing is a given, where hoping for something better will only set them up for more pain. Often, they dress, look, and act the part—droopy, dull, and disinterested.

FAMOUS FACES

Sylvia Plath was a writer in love with death. In her novel *The Bell Jar,* written when she was in her twenties, she describes her life as a "Type A" kid who won a guest editorship at *Mademoiselle* magazine. What would have been a coup for many a girl in the 1950s was an experience filled with disappointment and pain. When she came home, she was so curious about death that she dispassionately planned her own suicide. She was discovered by her mother before she succeeded, and it was not until she was 39 years old that her romance with death was consummated. Even then, it was more an adolescent fascination she'd never outgrown than a deliberate attempt. She had turned on the gas in her stove before her maid arrived. Unfortunately, the maid came to the door too late.

In *The Fragile Alliance: An Orientation to the Psychiatric Treatment of the Adolescent,* I wrote about the cold, aloof mother of a fourteen-year-old delinquent "nay-saying" girl, who, on the surface, seemed not to care about her daughter at all. But during her first therapy session she cried continuously, complaining that her daughter's problems were all her fault. She said she had been in a state of shock when she learned about her daughter's delinquency. "I guess I thought someone was going to come and arrest me," she said.

This is a telling example of "like mother, like daughter." As with this troubled fourteen-year-old whose mother herself was on the edge, kids who view themselves as "nay-saying" losers usually come from depressed families, from homes where the message is despair. They can be children who have been sexually or physically abused, children of alcoholic parents, children who have inherited their parent's biological depression, or simply extremely sensitive children who have learned to fear their intense responses to the outside world. When these teens don't receive the love and support they need in early childhood, they grow up empty, without any self-esteem and without hope.

The type of depression "nay-sayers" suffer from is called chronic neurotic depression, which will be discussed at length later on in this chapter; you'll see that there are good reasons for their actions and feelings.

3. Learning-Disabled Teens

Many "nay-saying" losers are also learning-disabled. In fact, teenagers with learning disabilities make up a high percentage of psychiatric cases.

It makes sense. Take the example of Billy, a 13-year-old. He was always behind in his reading assignments in school. He couldn't understand what he was supposed to read. This led to boredom and frustration. Soon he was acting out in class, and his reading level dropped even lower. In his mind, he was really trying. He wanted to be good. But all the adults around him labeled him a troublemaker. From his parents to his teachers, everyone thought he was bad. Soon Billy stopped trying. He didn't expect to succeed—and he was right.

Today, educators and parents are much more aware of learning disabilities in the young. They can be caught earlier, and the victims can be helped. (In Chapter Six, we will go over learning disabilities in more detail.)

Unfortunately, many learning-disabled kids have already learned the loser's dismal view of life before entering adolescence. For them, there are two problems to overcome: disability and depression.

4. Juvenile Delinquents

Listen to this dialogue from *A Fragile Alliance* between a therapist and a 16-year-old boy who always lit a cigarette before his session began:

> BOY: You mean I can't even smoke in this crummy office?
>
> DOCTOR: I didn't say there was a rule against it. I just noticed that you never talk about smoking, yet you light up the moment you sit in that chair.
>
> BOY: So what?
>
> DOCTOR: So we're here to understand why you do the things you do.
>
> BOY: Because I want to, okay?
>
> DOCTOR: Well, if you want to go through a session standing on your head and playing a harmonica, I guess that's okay, but I'd probably ask you why you wanted to.
>
> BOY: (*Grinning*) Are you going to tell my parents that I smoke in here?
>
> DOCTOR: We can talk about that in a minute, but I wonder why you're doing something here that you know your parents disapprove of.
>
> BOY: (*Seriously*) Yeah, I know I shouldn't smoke. It would kill my parents if they knew. I don't know why I'm always bad.
>
> DOCTOR: I don't think it's going to help to criticize yourself. Let's try to understand what's really going on here.
>
> BOY: Well, I kinda wanted to see what you'd say about the smoking.

This boy suffers from conduct disorder. Like many other teenagers, he translates his fears of dependency and the world at large into action. But for juvenile delinquents, that action is self-destructive. Rather than confront a "shameful" vulnerability, they affect a tough veneer.

In addition to the strange new emotions all teenagers face, many juvenile delinquents also carry around a rigid, unyielding conscience—a primitive superego that will not allow them to "try on" their new feelings and impulses. Guilt-ridden and

ashamed, these teens can express themselves only if they stick
on a self-inflicted punishment. Believing that it's "okay to sin a
little—or a lot—if I promise to die tomorrow," they become
hell-bent on self-destruction. Unfortunately, this can mean failure in school, violence, and drug addiction. Underneath all this
is a very sad youngster. (We will discuss more on juvenile
delinquency in Part II.)

5. The Overprotected Child
Sometimes the problem isn't too little love but too much.
Consider the case of Sally, an overweight fourteen-year-old girl.
Sally's parents doted on her. An only child born late in her
parents' lives, she received all the nurturing that her parents
had stored up over the years. Sally was wonderful. She was
beautiful, talented, and smart.

As Sally approached adolescence, her self-esteem was in
place. She knew she was loved by her parents; she believed she
was as terrific as they said she was. Unfortunately, as Sally
began the almost instinctual push towards independence, she
found no safe arena to regain her self-esteem. The kids at school
called her "Tubby." Her teachers consistently gave her Cs.
Instead of a shining star, she became a total eclipse—withdrawing
further and further into herself. Without any positive feedback
in the outside world, she went backward, back to her parents
where she knew she was safe. Rather than self-discovery and
growth, Sally found stagnation. She began to resent her parents—
they had lied to her about her abilities. But she was too
guilt-ridden and needy to vocalize her anger. Instead, she began
to eat more and more. . . .

Parents must learn to love and let go. Overprotection is but
another route on an adolescent's journey down to depression.

6. The Loner
John, at eighteen, was an excellent student. But outside of his
studies, he had few interests. He spent most of his time in his
room. He had no friends his age. Instead he enjoyed talking to
his parent's friends whenever they came over for dinner. He
was about to graduate high school, but he had no idea what to
do with his life. Rather than experience the world around him,

he embroidered fantastical adolescent dreams that grew more and more outrageous with time. He would imagine himself elected head of the country without ever running for office. He would tell his parents and their friends that he wanted to do something meaningful, but he couldn't find anything short of "reconstructing the Executive Branch of the United States government."

Loners like John live in an unreal world. They believe that everything would be simple if only their parents, their school, their country, their world was different. They see no place where their talents can flourish. Consequently, they plunge deeper and deeper into themselves, refusing to reach out, refusing to try. Instead, they form unrealistic goals that are virtually impossible to reach. In their minds, it is easier to blame an outside "devil" than confront the terrifying demons of change inside themselves. When these excuses fail, they become depressed.

As you can see, depression can grow in many soils. It is a complex, multifaceted disease that has many causes and many expressions. A crisis situation can either cause depression or be merely a manifestation of a disease that has been lying dormant. Learning-disabled teenagers can become depressed, but their depression could have taken root in the soil of biological vulnerability even before formal education was introduced. Chemically addicted teenagers could have turned to drugs because they were depressed—and learning-disabled. Type A kids caught in a "failing" situation could have a personality disorder that stems from a chemical imbalance in the brain. Like the chicken and the egg, it is sometimes difficult to determine which came first—the situation or the depression.

That's why only a professional can sort out the multiple sources of depression—and apply specific treatments that will work.

THE EXPRESSIONS

A normal depressive mood doesn't last too long. Backed by love, understanding, and their own natural resiliency, most teenagers are soon back in the swing of things. But when an adolescent's depression is no longer a mood but has a life force of its own, outside help is needed. Once depressive illness occurs in a teenager, it usually has one of three basic expressions. Each one can be cured—if parents can recognize their child's cries:

Face 1: The Slings of Fate, or, Reactive Depressions

A move to another state. A failing grade. A mother and father constantly fighting with each other. The death of a parent or grandparent. Any of these alone or in concert can set a reactive depression in motion. Caused by external situations, set into motion by loss, this depressive face is usually temporary—unless it is ignored or minimized. It finds fertile ground to grow in the following situations.

Relocation

My cousin, a computer whiz, has had to move his family three times in the last few years because of business. When I asked one of his daughters if the newest move was hard on her, she answered, "Not this one. I'm older and used to it by now. I'm kind of looking forward to it. But Alabama was a different story." I turned to her father and asked him what it was like. His reply: "I'll tell you. There wasn't a sound in the car as we drove, except for this voice from the backseat that would occasionally say, 'I hate you, father. I hate you, father...'"

Moving is considered one of the major reasons for stress in today's adult world. But when it comes to kids, its impact is greatly underestimated. To a teenager, a move means a significant loss—not just from a few best friends, but from an entire comforting and familiar support network. This uprooting can easily translate into reactive depression.

Despite good intentions, parents can unwittingly add fuel to this depression's fire. It's hard for them to focus on their teenager's pain when they too are feeling stressed—and full of guilt. Instead, they try to stop their kids from expressing their feelings of loss and fear with words of encouragement: "Oh, you're gonna love this new place. It's great. School will be terrific. Stop talking that way—you're upsetting your sister." They don't want to hear how their son will miss his friends, how their daughter spent the whole night in tears. It only makes them feel worse—and adds to their guilt. Unfortunately, this attitude only magnifies a teenager's isolation and loss. Parents would do more good if they shared their own thoughts and fears about the move with their kids. Everyone would feel better— and reactive depression might not come to roost. Generally speaking, the rule of thumb is "Grieve the loss now, avoid the depression later."

Rites of Passage

There she was, confident and proud in her cap and gown. As valedictorian of her graduating class, Jennifer stood at the podium, smiling at her classmates, her beaming parents, her friends and neighbors gathered in the June noonday sun. She began to speak the opening lines of the speech she'd been rehearsing for weeks. Suddenly, her voice started to tremble. Her eyes filled up. Her cap fell off as she ran off the stage in tears. . . .

Graduation can be a traumatic time for teenagers, especially from a high school they have known and loved, a place where their support network was in full force. It is an event fraught with reactive depression traps.

So too is college. It can be an exciting environment, as well as a frightening, unfamiliar one. Consider Josh, a freshman who spent his entire first semester lying on his dorm room bed. If he hadn't had the help of the school's counseling service, he would have missed the opportunity of a lifetime. He would have flunked out—and stayed mired in depression.

Other teenagers might do well all through college, only to plunge when they find themselves entering the job market. The real world can hold some rude surprises, especially when a bright, successful, and popular college student finds him or herself on the corporate ladder's bottom rung.

Rites of passage are a necessary part of growing up, an exhilarating time of completion and discovery. But they can also be a ritual of vulnerability, loss . . . and depression.

Wounded Pride

Everyone agreed: Susan, Ruth, and Judy had to be the most

popular girls in school. They had steady boyfriends. They always wore the styles seen in last month's *Seventeen*. They even got straight As on Mr. McLean's English tests. But one afternoon, Judy had a fight with Susan in the cafeteria. It seemed Judy had decided to compete for Student Council president, even though the trio had agreed that Susan would run. In less than twenty-four hours, the word had gone out. Judy was stuck up. She was ostracized by her three closest friends, her boyfriend, and by the other kids who counted. Her world began to fall apart. . . .

The adolescent world is filled with rejection. From almost daily school exams to fickle friendships, from parental judgments to dateless Junior Proms—teenagers are constantly accosted by wounds to their egos. And because they have not yet learned to cushion these blows, they can quickly spiral down into a severe reactive depression.

Illness

Bill had been a diabetic ever since he was five years old. When he was younger, it didn't matter as much. Except for the insulin shots his mother gave him daily, he had a fairly normal life. But now, as a teenager, his diabetes was different. He was different. When he turned down shakes, candy bars, and ice cream, the other kids either looked at him with sympathy—or they looked the other way. He couldn't try out for football like the other guys, and he had no dates. He felt like a freak. His insulin syringe became a daily reminder that he was strange— different and defective.

Teenagers want to be accepted. To be saddled with difference can be extremely painful. Chronic illness is a common cause of depression in adults. It makes sense that chronically ill adolescents, with their added self-doubt and insecurity, would be prime candidates for depression.

Reactive depression can be dangerous for its victims. Filled with self-hatred and fear, many depressed teenagers find an out in drugs or violence. Because it is crisis-oriented, this depressive face can come without warning—and end in a successful suicide attempt.

To be forewarned is to be forearmed. There are usually warnings. Small signs of withdrawal, changes in mood, loss of interest—none of these should be ignored. They may be merely temporary ups and downs, but they can also be serious. And the good news is that, if recognized, reactive depressions can be easily cured, never to return.

Face 2: Remembrances of Things Past, or, Chronic Neurotic Depression

Sean was fifteen when he came to the psychiatric hospital. A bedwetter until he was eleven, Sean had a history of playing with matches and random destructiveness. He was sullen, unhappy, and full of mistrust. It made sense. When Sean's parents divorced, his mother refused custody. His father grudgingly accepted him, but had him hospitalized after he tried to commit suicide. Sean made some encouraging strides in therapy, but when I recommended long-term outpatient treatment, his father said that "Sean did not deserve to have another penny spent on his meanness."

Sean's world was a bleak one. He had learned early in life that the people he loved could not be trusted. He developed a chronic neurotic depression, which had nothing to do with external events or with the ups and downs of his adolescent years.

Some teenagers, like Sean, fall prey to depression way before puberty begins. In 1967, a study by Dr. Sandor Lorand showed that kids who crave affection as adolescents had not been adequately nourished in infancy. Their pain was internalized, translating into a low self-esteem and an aura of hopelessness that stayed with them as they grew up. In 1978, Dr. Kay Tooley reported similar findings in *The Journal of Orthopsychiatry*, also showing that though these teens might blame their school, their friends, their parents, or any other outside force, their problem was really deep within themselves.

"Hopeless and helpless. Yeah, I guess that's me"—John, 17

A negative outlook: More than anything else, teenagers suffering from chronic neurotic depression view life as hopeless and cheerless—and themselves as helpless to change it. They are true pessimists, always expecting the worst, which, more times than not, becomes a self-fulfilling prophecy. These depressed teens believe that:

- Nothing they ever do will change things—or change the way they feel.
- Life is an enemy, ready to run them down.
- The worst will always happen—a preoccupation that sets them up for failure. . . .
- And, when the worst does happen, it was probably their fault.
- A clean bill of health is a lie.
- Their bad self-image is an accurate appraisal of their bodies and their minds.

"Every time something good happens, it gets snatched away"
—Sandy, 15

Why hope for something that will never come true? Why think something good will happen when it never does? Chronic neurotic depressed teens avoid encouragement because they are terrified they'll be let down—again. Unfortunately, their fear becomes reality. Take the example of Jeanine, a young depressed teen. She thought she was fat, though she was actually five pounds below normal. She thought she was ugly, though she had beautiful green eyes and clear skin. Whenever a boy asked her out on a date, Jeanine grew anxious. She would start creating negative scripts in her mind: he would come to the door and laugh at her, he would ignore her at the dance, he would call at the last minute and stand her up. By the time Saturday night rolled around, Jeanine was so defensive that she jumped at the boy's every comment and every gesture. She was never asked out a second time, and her worst fears always came true.

"I could never get angry. I'm too afraid"—Bill, 16

This makes sense: If chronically depressed teens are terrified of rejection, they can never speak out. If they cannot cope with the world, they try to hide from it. If they feel their emotions are out of control, they can never get angry or confront anyone or anything head on.

The constricting fear these adolescents face comes from their childhoods—either from early rejection or from the intense way they reacted to stimuli from the outside world.

"I know my mother's disappointed in me, but I don't know why"—June, 14

As we have seen, young children get their self-esteem from their parents. When a mother shows her love to her child, her beaming face is like a mirror. Her smile is reflected onto her baby, who immediately sees that he or she is worthwhile. This process, called "mirroring" by Dr. Heinz Kohut, is an important seed of self-esteem.

Unfortunately, many chronically depressed teens never saw a positive mirror image reflected in their parent's gaze. Maybe their mothers or fathers were depressed themselves, unable to smile or respond to their baby. Maybe their mothers or fathers were so anxious about parenting, they couldn't relax enough to show their love. Consequently, these teens never develop a healthy self-esteem. They never find a "shiny" reflection that says: "I'm cute. I'm worthwhile. I am loved." Instead, these kids grow up empty and unsure, filled with a nagging sense that they didn't do what they were supposed to do—and that they just don't measure up.

Unfortunately, if one or both parents are depressed, the chances are good that their children will be, too. Their children identify with their parents' blighted view of life and repeat the pattern.

Though chronic neurotic depression is difficult to cure, it can be treated. Through patience, therapy, and skill training, troubled teenagers can be taught to replace their fear with hope.

Face 3: It's Not All in the Mind, or, Major Affective Disorders
Craig was an active child. He was bright and disarming, and he always took center stage when he toddled into a room. He would sometimes be quiet for hours at end, but his parents took little notice. He was tired. He had a slight virus. But as Craig

grew older, his mood swings fluctuated more and more. Though his friends also jumped from mood to mood, his were more pronounced. In college, when he was high, he'd have night-long poker games in his dorm room, where, more times than not, he lost his month's allowance. He'd strut around campus, charming the coeds and talking a mile a minute. But these highs were countered by very severe lows, with days on end when he wouldn't get out of bed. The evening he tried to kill himself, his parents brought him in to the hospital. He was diagnosed as suffering from manic-depressive illness, or bipolar affective disorder.

Depression can be biochemical, a physiological malfunctioning of the chemical messengers in the brain. The result can be, as in Craig's case, a manic-depressive illness. However, not all biological depressive illness is bipolar. Some patients have episodes of depression, but are never manic or euphoric.

Chemical imbalance is also implicated in many psychotic illnesses. Some of these illnesses, even many previously diagnosed as schizophrenic, are turning out to be atypical examples of mood disorders, responsive to the medications used for other bipolar or unipolar depressions. In all these cases where chemical imbalances play a major role, medication is necessary as part of the treatment. Today, tremendous strides have been made in this arena; we will learn about them later on.

We have examined some of the many faces depressed adolescents show the world. We have seen the why and the how that depression can be expressed. But without recognizing the actual symptoms of adolescent depression, a parent can miss important cues. Let's go on to those symptoms and examine how they are sometimes hidden.

CHAPTER FOUR

The Cry for Help: Symptoms of Adolescent Depression

"Not knowing what to do/Is it coming closer to you"

—*Alan, 18**

- Lately, Rose has been sleeping her weekends away. At first, her almost constant catnaps were a family joke, but now her sleepiness is getting more and more pronounced.

- When Ellis found out that his parents were getting a divorce, he ran into his room and slammed the door. He refused to come out or communicate. After all, the divorce was all his fault—and he was a horrible person. He couldn't stop blaming himself. . . .

- Whenever Abbie started a diet, she showed amazing discipline for at least two weeks before gobbling everything in sight. But this time, she's been on a diet for months—and eating less and less. . . .

- Joe has always been a withdrawn boy. Sensitive and shy, he was most comfortable reading and listening to music alone in his room. But lately, he's been staring at the ceiling—and thinking about death. . . .

- Billy quit the football team after finally making varsity. He says he's no longer interested.

*from "When Adolescents Write: Semiotics and Social Dimensions of Adolescents' Personal Writing" by B.E. Litowitz and R.A. Gundlach. In *Adolescent Psychiatry: Development and Clinical Studies, Volume 14*. Chicago: University of Chicago Press, 1987.

From irritability to excessive guilt, from weight change to suicidal thoughts—the symptoms of adolescent depression are as painful as its adult counterpart. Unfortunately, they are not as easily read.

THE SEVEN SYMPTOMS OF ADOLESCENT DEPRESSION

We don't have all the answers. There are as many different faces of adolescent depression as there are individual teens. But there are certain symptoms that come up time and again when a teenager is depressed. These seven basic symptoms can provide clues to your own child's mental health. Let's go over each of them, one by one.

1. A Loss of Interest
Once upon a time, your teenager loved school. But lately he has stopped studying. He just doesn't care. Or maybe your daughter is still studying just as hard as she always did, but she can't seem to concentrate and her grades have slipped. Whether it's school, sports, hanging out with friends, or simply shopping on a Saturday afternoon, a loss of interest in activities your teenager used to love is one of the most common signs of adolescent depression.

Parent Lookout Sign
Any change in your teenager's activity pattern that seems illogical to you.

2. Change in Mood
All adolescents change with the wind. When good things happen, a teenager is as high as a kite. When bad things happen, it's the end of the world. It's all a part of that inner instability, that transition between a self-esteem based on parental approval and one based on a general sense of competence in the larger world. But a long-term mood change is *not* normal—it is a major symptom of depression. Depressed teens may become irritable and angry, stomping furiously around the house and slamming doors. Or they might become withdrawn and sad, unable to let their anger show because they have always tried to

be "nice." But try to talk to these withdrawn teens and they'll snarl and snap—just like their short-fused, stomping counterparts.

Parent Lookout Sign

A display of sad, cranky, irritable, or irrational behavior in your teen.

3. Sleep Disturbance

When adults get depressed, chances are they will toss and turn all night long, waking up at odd hours and feeling the awful results of their sleepless night throughout the next day. But for depressed adolescents, the scenario is usually just the opposite: they will suffer from *hypersomnia*, sleeping much more than usual but feeling tired all the time.

Have you ever tried to wake a depressed teen in the morning? It's almost impossible. They not only sleep soundly when they hit the pillow, but once they do get up, they'll spend the day with their heads in a fog, their concentration nil. And, just like their adult counterparts, they'll start to feel better as the day progresses. Unfortunately, parents usually blame this pattern on staying up too late the night before. The depressed teens, too, look outside themselves for the source of their problem. They might complain that they are tired all the time because people expect too much from them . . . Their schoolwork is too heavy a load . . . Their parents are bringing them down . . . Not so. In actuality, a depressed teen is suffering from a tremendous amount of internal fatigue—an abnormal tiredness.

Parent Lookout Sign

A teen who can't get up in the morning, who complains about being tired all day, and who drags his or her feet continuously.

4. Weight Change

A teenage boy becomes an eating machine, gobbling up everything in sight. A teenage girl stops eating altogether, seemingly surviving on diet cola and crackers. Weight loss or weight gain is often a symptom of adolescent depression, and sometimes both are present. In bipolar depression, teenagers will overeat when in their depressive phases and eat virtually nothing during their manic highs.

Parent Lookout Sign
Any change of eating habits in your teen.

5. Movement Disturbances
Inner instability breeds discontent, especially for depressed teens. Because they are constantly going back and forth between feelings of stupidity and grandeur, between believing they can't do anything and believing they can do *everything*, their emotions will be erratic, and their movements will reflect these changing moods. Some depressed adolescents will start their mornings feeling lethargic and heavy, only to become agitated and fidgety as night approaches. Others will be agitated and nervous in the afternoon, but begin and end each day in slow motion.

Parent Lookout Sign
A teen whose movements and action are changeable and erratic, especially at different times of the day.

6. Excessive Guilt Feelings
Minor sexual misbehavior. A parent's failed marriage. An imagined misdeed. From "bad" things they believe they have done to embarrassing scenarios that are all in their heads, depressed teens will feel excessively guilty—and excessively at fault. They might:

- Think they made a fool of themselves in front of their peers or important adults.
- Take responsibility for bad things that happen to other family members.
- Imagine that a situation is much worse than it is—or create it out of thin air.
- Obsessively think about the situation and its outcome.

Parent Lookout Sign
Any change in your teenager's attitudes about school, friends, and him or herself—especially accompanied by withdrawal, sadness, self-reproachment, and obsessive conversation.

7. Suicidal Tendencies

A troubled boy will only ask for help indirectly. Instead of talking about his pain, he'll show it—by acting out, by retreating, by becoming a stranger in his own home. To him, a cry for help is a sign of weakness, especially because he tends to do things in packs with other boys. A teenage boy might not attempt suicide as often as a girl, but if he does, he is three times more likely to succeed.

A depressed girl, on the other hand, will be more open in asking for help. She will easily discuss her feelings with her friends. But even she might avoid the issue. Even she can become entrapped in the complexities of her pain. In fact, a teenage girl is likely to attempt suicide three times more than a boy, but she is much less likely to die as a result.

The cruel, hard reality is that depressed people do think about death, and teenagers are no exception. It is very common for a depressed adolescent to be preoccupied with the idea of death—from thoughts of self-injury to plans for self-punishment.

Parent Lookout Sign

Any suggestion or reference to death and suicide by your teen *must* be taken seriously. Because of its magnitude in today's world, I will be discussing teenage suicide in depth in Chapter Seven.

MASTERS OF DISGUISE

Unfortunately, understanding the seven basic symptoms of adolescent depression is not enough. If you still find it difficult to recognize your teenager's depression, you are in good company. Believe it or not, it is only within the last twenty years or so that major depressive illnesses in teens have been diagnosed. Unlike adult depression, the faces depressed adolescents wear are easily camouflaged, concealed by seven masks that hide the symptoms of depression from their family, their friends—and themselves. In order for you to detect your teenager's symptoms, you must take off the masks.

Disguise # 1: Ordinary Life

As we have seen, adolescence is a time of transition, of self-discovery, and of breaking away. What looks like depression might very well be the normal ups and downs of growing up. How do you tell the difference? Take note of the duration and severity of your child's symptoms. Trust your instincts. Try to communicate. And don't hesitate to seek professional advice.

Disguise # 2: Avoiding Dependency

"I feel real bad. I need your help"—If only parents could hear these words when their teen is depressed. Unfortunately, a direct request for help is seldom heard. Because they are trying to break away from their parents, they'll avoid reaching out like the plague. To their minds, it's a move back to childhood, to that "awful" dependency they are instinctively trying to escape. Depressed teens will even avoid recognizing the need for help in themselves. Instead, they'll do a lot of whistling in the dark, putting up a false front and pretending they can handle something even when they can't. Their troubled souls stay hidden from the world.

Disguise #3: Mislabeling

Adults have knowledge that can only come from experience—at least enough to determine why they are feeling low. Not so adolescents. They can't see that they are depressed. They can only blame their problems on outside events. To teens, action is paramount, and patience a disease. They want to plunge in and change things, but this can be a curse as well as a blessing. Certainly, teens need to be involved, to learn, and to participate in activities, but this drive to *do* instead of question can make it hard for them—and their parents—to realize that they are depressed. Instead of saying, "I feel depressed," a depressed teen will say, "I'm bored. There's nothing to do." If you ask teens outright if they are depressed, they'll say, "Yeah, 'cause school is such a drag. I hate it." They are completely unaware that the source of their problem is depression—and that any place and any activity would look drab and uninteresting to them.

Disguise #4: Substituting Excitement

As soon as teenagers begin to feel depressed, they begin to crave action and excitement. There's nothing like anxiety or fear to keep teens "one step ahead" of their pain. Unfortunately, this is a time when many teens start experimenting with drugs, a common but dangerous way to cover up symptoms of depression. (We will go over the link between drugs and teenage depression in the next chapter.)

Disguise #5: Overachievement

Because teenagers have such a hard time identifying their depression, they'll sometimes conclude that they are feeling bad because they are unworthy, not as good as others. Their solution? Doing more and more, and trying to excel in every facet of their lives. These are the "Type A" kids discussed in Chapter Three, the overachievers who stay one step ahead of their depression by doing better than anyone else. Only then can they prove to themselves that they are worthy. As we have also seen, these kids live on a precarious tightrope. They can feel terrific only as long as they achieve. One minor slip and they spiral down.

Disguise #6: Parents Are People, Too

No parents like to see their children in pain. If a mother had been a "belle" in her youth, she won't want to accept the fact that her daughter is not going out on any dates. If a father had his heart set on his son becoming a football star, he'll turn away from the fact that his youngster is a klutz. The same goes with depression. Parents don't want to see that their teen is depressed, and they might ignore the signs. Further, they could be depressed themselves, and unable to see beyond their own pain.

Disguise #7: Family Ties

There is safety in numbers, and a bond found in groups that is difficult to sever. Nowhere is this more evident than in families, the most primal and elemental group in existence. Families, as a whole, strive to maintain a balance. They have an instinctual "pecking order," where everybody has a place—and stays there.

Anything that shakes up that balance threatens the continuation of the group, and that includes all kinds of change. Families will only accept gradual transitions, and these must be slow in coming. Even normal adolescents, gradually changing from dependent children to independent adults, will feel their family's tug as they slowly pull away. Triple the feel of that family tug for depressed adolescents. They are frozen in their transition, placed in a family-made "pressure cooker" where they can't express their pain for fear of destroying the status quo. Families, in turn, will sweep their teen's depression under the rug rather than admit they need to make some changes. The depression is simply too radical, too painful, and too outside the norm for many families to face. Instead, they'll put on a good front, saying "We'll manage" or "Everything's fine." Meanwhile, the depression gets buried in the family plot, more and more hidden from view. . . .

We have now journeyed through the world of adolescence—from typical behavior to the many faces depressed teens wear. We have seen the signs and symptoms of adolescent depression as well as the ways they are sometimes concealed.

But our journey is not yet over. There are still roadblocks up ahead before we reach a cure. In the next section, I'll be discussing the very real problems faced by adolescents—and their parents—in today's complex world.

PART II
A Mirror Cracked

CHAPTER FIVE

Drugs: The Temptation and the Curse

"I was a happy little blind lady."

*—mother of teenage addict**

Fact: Since 1977, teenage death rates have steadily increased—from drug overdoses, drug-induced accidents, and drug-related suicides.

Fact: Ninety percent of all high school graduates have smoked marijuana at least once. Sixty percent had their first experience between sixth and ninth grades.

Fact: Among cigarette-smoking high school students, close to 75 percent have tried to quit—unsuccessfully.

Fact: Adults need between four and five years to become addicted to a drug. Teenagers need only 15.5 months.

Fact: Boys with alcoholic fathers have four to five times more chance of developing alcoholism themselves.

Fact: Drugs today are deadly, more potent and more damaging than the drugs sold on the streets just twenty years ago.

Yes, drugs are serious business. And despite the Reagan administration's "Just Say No" campaign, despite the bad press given drugs like crack, PCP, and cocaine, despite the fact that teens are more aware than ever before—adolescents continue to do drugs. Across racial, economic, and social lines, drugs and teens are still "dirty dancing," with more and more deadly results.

*from *The Fragile Alliance*, 3rd edition. By John Meeks, M.D. Malabar, Florida: Robert E. Krieger Publishing, 1986.

WHY DRUGS?

A teenage patient of mine who successfully got off drugs once told me, "In a very real sense, I'm a lot happier than I ever was on drugs. But nothing will ever give me the intensity of pleasure that cocaine did."

Drugs seduce—especially among vulnerable teenagers. Almost every teenager today has tried at least one drug, either in a "take it or leave it" social situation, in a more deliberate, curious experimental fashion, or in a more uncontrollable manner that leads to problems and addiction. Unfortunately, it's almost impossible to define the lines between the three arenas.

From alcohol to cocaine, drugs are easy to find if a teen wants to try them, but availability is only part of the picture. They have always been the scourge of society. In the late 1800s, the drug problem was so serious that a teaching supervisor at an Illinois university was prompted to complain about "the widespread inhaling of chloroform by high school students." Add the vast array of medical elixirs filled with opium that were hawked at the time, and you have people becoming addicts at a very early age.

Drugs are a seductive danger to teens—especially troubled teens—because they offer:

- A "magic spell" to stay safe in a turbulent world where they can't trust anyone, including themselves
- A form of control while they struggle through the transition of leaving their parents and their dependency ties
- Ways to "stay one step ahead" of those fears and anxieties that crop up in the adolescent years
- A tempting chance to feel good and get a sense of belonging.

In fact, it is this sense of belonging that more times than not triggers that first joint or pill. I have found that social, economic, and lifestyle ties are surprisingly unimportant when it comes to trying drugs. *But peer pressure is important.* Rather than thinking what will happen to them, kids wonder if their friends are doing it. And the more ridicule or threats they receive for saying no, the more they'll be pressured to join in. Proof is seen in a study done by Drs. Chewing and Lindner in 1984 which showed that 30 percent of all high school students were pressed to have a cigarette or a drink by their friends. Only strong religious ties, conservative political convictions and positive college plans can stop this peer pressure in its tracks.

Teens will also join in because they overestimate the number of people who smoke or drink or do drugs. "Everyone's doing it" is something they truly believe.

But inner city or outback country, there is truth to these words and their inference that environment plays a role in drugs. When teens watch their parents deal with their day-to-day stress by smoking or drinking or taking a joint, it reinforces their belief that "everyone—even my parents—are doing it. Why can't I?"

WHY ADDICTION?

Listen to this dialogue between a 16-year-old drug-dependent boy from a middle-class home and his psychiatrist at Fair Oaks Hospital in New Jersey:

> DOCTOR: How old were you when you first started using any drugs?
> GARY: Nine.
> DOCTOR: What did you start with?
> GARY: Reefer.
> DOCTOR: Okay. Can you give me a list of all the drugs you've used, Gary?
> GARY: Pot. Coke. Crack. Mescaline. Acid. Speed. Crystal meth. Smack. Base. Dust. Sometimes alcohol . . . *

Like the chicken and the egg, it's difficult to say which came first—the depression or the drugs. In some cases, the drugs lead to depression. Take this example of a patient I treated as medical director of the Psychiatric Institute of Montgomery County:

Ellis was a sophomore at a nearby university who wanted to

*From *Crack: What You Should Know About the Cocaine Epidemic* by Calvin Chatlos, M.D. and Lawrence D. Chilnick, New York: Perigee Books, 1987.

drop out. When I first met him, he was the epitome of a depressed teenager—withdrawn, pale, tired, and unkempt. He'd been seeing a therapist for six months with no improvement. The first thing I did was a differential diagnosis to make sure his depression was not a symptom of some other disease. His urine test showed traces of THC, the ingredient found in marijuana. When I asked him about this, Ellis confessed that he smoked five joints a day. When he stopped, his depression went away almost immediately.

But in other cases, drugs can hide an underlying depression, usually of a chronic neurotic nature. These teens turn to drugs to alleviate their pain, but the drugs ultimately make their depression worse because:

- If teens take stimulants like cocaine or speed, then withdrawal plunges them into physiological depression.
- If teens take depressants like marijuana, alcohol, or "downers," the chemicals immediately go to work on the central nervous system, producing both an emotional and biochemical depressive reaction. These drugs produce an initial euphoric sense of release as the drug's blood level rises, then depression as the drug starts to wear off.
- Kids on drugs do lots of things that they can feel guilty about—from stealing money from their parents to vandalizing and worse—which will make them feel even more depressed.
- The drug scene itself is not exactly a nurturing one. It involves deceit and secretiveness that destroys the supportive, helpful relationships of caring parents, other adults, and "straight" peers.

The reasons why some teens become addicted varies from individual to individual. Heredity plays a role. Studies show that the tendency to addiction can be inherited from one's parents. For example, studies show that adopted sons have a four to five times greater risk of becoming alcoholics if their natural father had been one—even if they had been adopted at an early age and had never lived with their natural parents.

Another study found that there was a 54 percent chance of one identical twin becoming an addict if the other one already was.

Sometimes it's the gene pool that determines addiction. In 1985, Drs. Robins and Alessi discovered that depressives have a sensitivity to chemicals, combined with a limited tolerance. Depressed teens born with this sensitivity might be drawn to drugs, only to find that they have quickly become addicts, needing more and more to get high.

Like math or English, addictive behavior can also be learned. Dr. Miller Newton studied how the use of drugs can stimulate an addictive response. He found that teenagers who are drawn to drugs enjoy the high at first. But as tolerance grows, so does antisocial behavior, such as withdrawal, vandalism, rudeness, and hostility. Their growing minds and bodies stop developing in constructive ways. Lack of proper rest and nutrition keep their bodies soft. Their memories lag, their concentration falls, and they lose interest in the world around them. Soon, these teens begin to cling to their drugs in desperation—their only source of comfort. They learn that addiction is necessary to maintain a sense of self-esteem.

DRUG TALK: Some of the Drugs Teenagers Take

1. PCP or Phencyclidine or Angel Dust.
This drug promotes hallucinogenic, psychotic behavior and numbness. Teens on PCP will act impulsively, including attempting suicide.

2. Marijuana or Grass.
Today, marijuana is ten times stronger than it was in the sixties. Some youngsters seem to use it in a limited way without harmful effects. Other kids on grass will display an inability to concentrate and remember; in some cases, this amotivational "burnout" leads to lethargy and depression, which can result in suicidal thoughts or actions.

3. Alcohol.
Unfortunately, liquor is legal and widely available—but it *is* a drug. Alcohol causes more automobile deaths—both

accidental and suicidal—than any other drug. Blood level samples taken at the time of death prove that half of all teenage suicide victims died while intoxicated. Long-term heavy use of alcohol almost always leads to a state of depression.

4. Cocaine.

Today, people have become savvy to this drug's addictive capabilities. It used to be very expensive and not easily accessible to teens. Although the price of cocaine has decreased, it can still be expensive as the amount of cocaine consumed increases. Combining the pricey nature of cocaine with cocaine's stimulant properties results in cocaine being the only drug that compels people to work. Other drugs induce addicts to quit work and withdraw, but not so cocaine. Long-term use leads to mucous membrane damage and severe withdrawal symptoms, including depression, paranoia, and lethargy. The "laziness" may be late in arriving, but it will come.

5. Crack.

It kills. This is *the* deadly drug that started a national campaign because, as a cocaine derivative, it has the same euphoric effects without the exorbitant price tag. But crack is so addictive so fast that it ultimately is more expensive than cocaine. The effects are so intense that, as with heroin, crack users want to be alone to get their rush.

6. Minor Tranquilizers.

Though these drugs were created to save lives, they too are abused, especially because teens tend to take drugs in combination with others. When they combine alcohol with Valium, for instance, they can go into a coma. Other prescription drugs can also cause problems. In fact, the most common drugs taken in suicidal overdoses are antidepressants, which is why medication must be carefully monitored when it is necessary in teenage depression therapy.

Learning disabilities are also a route to addiction. Learning-disabled teens will turn to drugs as a way to escape their feelings of inferiority and confusion. (In fact, learning disabilities, conduct disorders, abuse, and drug addiction are all bound together in depression's trap; we will discuss this link in the next chapter.)

Other factors that create addiction include life experience, social expectations, drug-taking frequency, and availability. One of the reasons why crack is so dangerous is that addiction occurs within three or four weeks, and it's inexpensive and readily available on the street.

THE SEDUCTION ELEMENT

It's easy to see why kids are drawn to drugs. At first, they seem to provide that "magic cure," keeping a teenager's embarrassing and painful dependency needs at bay. But ultimately drugs can never work. Like a full-blown devil exacting a price, the side effects eventually harm and interfere with that perfect "high." At the same time, tolerance is built up, and more of the drug is needed to get results. Soon, a teen is in a vicious cycle of addiction where:

- Larger doses create more harmful side effects, both emotionally and physically.
- The more harmful the side effects, the more teens cry out for drugs to stop the pain.
- The more drugs they take, the more harmful the side effects. . . .

Unfortunately, addiction increases the likelihood of depression, of those hopeless and helpless feelings of despair that can lead to suicide. In teens, this is even more cause for alarm, because adolescents are action-oriented, impulsive, and unable to put time into perspective. They just can't see the forest for the trees. They'll take the drugs now and worry about the consequences later. In fact, the emphasis in smoking prevention classes for teens is put on bad breath instead of lung cancer and heart disease.

Healthy teens might try a drug, but they will stop if:

- They can't get them any more.
- They receive parental disapproval.
- They have a minor scrape with the law.
- They recognize that the drugs are interfering with their long-range plans in life.

But teens in trouble not only won't stop—they *can't*.

SIGNS AND SYMPTOMS

What kind of teen uses drugs? Some are depressed, lonely, and inhibited, like the "nay-sayer" type of adolescent. For these teens, drugs are a key to the door of acceptance. They will free their inhibitions and calm their social anxiety.

Then there are the aggressive drug users, the teens who become grandiose and arrogant. They use drugs to keep their excitement level charged up, to maintain a sense of euphoria and have power over themselves and others.

There are also teenage drug-users hellbent on self-destruction. These kids have no regard for their own safety or survival. Like lemmings moving closer and closer to the cliff, they will take drug after drug until they fall.

But in the midst of these three generalized faces are individuals, teens from all walks of life, good teens and confused teens, sons and daughters who have become hooked on drugs. How can you tell if your teen is on drugs?

It's harder than you think. One of the ways drug counselors and medical professionals determine chemical dependency is through symptoms of drug withdrawal. But teens don't detoxify the same way as adults. First of all, they are reluctant to talk about their feelings. As we have learned in earlier chapters, they will only ask for help indirectly, preferring action to thought. Secondly, teens are highly resilient. Their youth helps them bounce back fast, and because they haven't been on drugs as long as their adult counterparts, their withdrawal symptoms will be less severe.

But observation can reveal a lot. *When drugs become more important than human interaction to teens, they are chemically addicted.* The more drugs teenagers use, the more they pull away from human contact. Because they see other people—especially their parents—as the dangerous, undependable, and hostile enemy, they will continue to escape through drugs. As we have seen, it is the addict's only way left to soften internal conflict and outside frustration.

If your child has begun to isolate himself, to be sensitive and hostile to others, it is possible that he or she is hooked on drugs. Let's go over some of the symptoms now:

Warning Signs
1. Withdrawal from family and friends
2. Erratic, irritable behavior
3. Loss of appetite
4. Dilated or red eyes
5. Activities dropped that your teenager used to love—without his or her filling the time with other equally constructive activities
6. A lack of ability to have fun
7. Few interests or hobbies
8. Relationship with others hostile, dishonest, and manipulative
9. Irresponsibility
10. Sniffling, runny nose
11. Self-neglect
12. Treating you the parent as the enemy, including yelling at you for no reason
13. Your inexplicable loss of money or valuables
14. Memory impairment
15. Drop in school grades and truancy
16. Chronic lying about where he or she has been
17. Physical evidence of drugs and drug paraphernalia
18. Change of friends
19. A "gut" feeling that you've lost your child.

Unfortunately, even seeing these symptoms are not enough because of one crucial factor...

Denial

It runs in families, and no one is immune. The addicted teens themselves will deny they have a problem. How can they say that drugs aren't working when that is all they have to keep the world at bay? When drugs are no longer in their control, they are filled with anxiety, which translates into more drugs and more denial. Think about it: When you set out to do something to avoid being dependent on people only to recognize the truth that it's made you *more* dependent, it's really hard to accept: "That's all I had! Now I have nothing!" This all-and-nothing stress makes teens reluctant to ever admit they are addicts. Instead, they'll say, "I can take it or leave it. No problem!"

But teens are not the only guilty ones. Parents, too, deny. I have seen parents of chemically addicted teenagers walk past a coffee table scattered with joints and not ever see them! Even if they notice the drugs and confront their teen, they will accept any answer, no matter how ludicrous: "Oh, yeah. That's Billy's stuff. He left it last week." I even know of a case where a boy had a drug fest for three days in the family basement, while his mother was upstairs, seemingly unaware of the crowd down below!

This behavior might seem embarrassing, but it is common. It's all part of that family balance I talked about in Chapter Four. Families want to sweep things under the rug. They don't want to acknowledge the stress that their teenager's drug habit is causing. They don't want to see things that will create a painful change. Let's face it: People don't like to confront painful situations until they are forced into it.

Unfortunately, this denial leads to "enabling," where, in the name of love, parents actually help their teens on their self-destructive paths. By looking the other way when their teen steals money from a drawer, by not seeing the drug paraphernalia in their daughter's room, by nodding their heads at whatever excuse their son gives for his overnight absence, parents enable the drug habit to continue—and get worse.

But there is treatment—and a cure.

THE TREATMENT AND THE CURE

At the Psychiatric Institute of Montgomery County in Maryland, we have found a high rate of success in treating drug-addicted teens with a program based on eight points:

1. Abstinence

Period. There is no halfway mark. As members of Alcoholics Anonymous say, "I am a *recovering* alcoholic"—not a recovered one. If smokers only wanted three cigarettes a day they would never think of quitting. If teens stopped after only one joint, they'd never become addicts. We cannot treat adolescents who are still talking drugs. They will only continue to deny their problems and refuse to understand that they are abusing drugs.

2. Family Involvement

Drug abuse is a family problem, and everyone in the family must be helped. From parents to older or younger brothers and sisters, all have felt the pain and the confusion of living with a drug-addicted teen. Families must learn:

- How they enabled the addicted teen to do drugs—so that it won't happen again.
- Ways to offer support and understanding that will really help the teen stay off drugs.
- How families might unconsciously sabotage a teen on the road to health, because they themselves feel depressed, angry, and threatened by this change in family balance.
- Ways to find relief from their own pain and heartache.

Family involvement begins with a . . .

3. Marathon Session

Here, all the families of all the new patients come together to talk about their experiences. For a whole day, they become educated, learning the concept of enabling and the right kinds of support. By sharing their experiences with others in the same boat, families see that they are not alone. They see others acting the same way they did, and they don't feel quite as stupid. "That's right! I did the same thing! Why did I do that?"

4. The Addicted Teen's Awareness That a Problem Exists

Because of their own denial, many teens refuse to see they are
sick, even if they come to us beaten, thin, and lacking any will
to live. These teens cling to their one "ace in the hole" until it
literally destroys them, unless we get them to face their addiction once and for all.

I remember one boy who attempted suicide while under the
influence of alcohol. He had taken everything from crack to
cocaine to Valium, and by the time he got to the Psychiatric
Institute, he was a walking zombie. Anyone could see he was an
addict in trouble—except for him. "Sure, I admit I got into
using too much for a while, Doc. I'll be the first to admit it. And
I know I've caused my family great unhappiness and I messed
up in school last year, but . . . I don't have to give it up. Sure, I
definitely have to cut back, I can't go on like this. But give it up
forever? Naw. . ."

These troubled teens genuinely believe what they are saying.
Denial is as powerful a drug as the drugs themselves. A
therapist must get beyond this denial and show these teens that
they are indeed addicts—and that there is a better way to life.

5. Control

To control total abstinence is crucial. If it is difficult to do on an
outpatient basis, we will hospitalize the teens for a time so that
the environment can be controlled. More times than not, when
these kids stop taking drugs, they begin to feel better and less
depressed once the withdrawal symptoms subside and they find
help in dealing with the problems drug use has created. The
sense of relief produces its own motivation for continuing to stay
"clean."

Sometimes a therapist will ask teens to stop just for a month
to get them motivated. Sometimes he or she will have the teens
sign contracts stating that they will stop taking drugs. And, at
the Psychiatric Institute, we use the following technique.

6. Peer Confrontation

Because peers have such an influence in getting a teen to try
drugs in the first place, they are equally as important in
implementing the cure. That's why we have group sessions with

peers who have been there—but are further down the road toward success. Here, when the drug-addicted teen says, "I don't really have to quit," there's another teen who can counter with, "Yeah, that's what I said, too—and I almost died." The healthier teens can anticipate the next rationalization before it comes—and they can commiserate because they were there:

> ADDICTED TEEN: I was crazy at the time. School was getting me down.
> HEALTHIER TEEN: Yeah, and I know what you're going to say next. You're gonna blame the whole thing on school, right? But that's not really true, is it. Not everybody gets where we were. . . .

These peers are not doctors or parents. They have no ax to grind. They are not trying to get something from the teen, who is already suspicious of all adults and mistrustful of the world. They are just kids—like the troubled teen. Not only that, but they are kids who are getting better—and enjoying it!

As one recovering drug addict said to me: "I thought I wouldn't want to give up drugs 'cause it was fun, but I'm having more fun! I realize now that drugs made me unhappy."

7. Long-Term Therapy

Habits die hard. Memories lose their harsh reality. And abstinence can get harder with time. Teens can:

- Forget they had a problem and start to deny again.
- Yearn for the drug-induced euphoria—especially when life gets rocky or when they are delving into painful areas in therapy.

Because of these factors, the skills a former teenage addict learned with us must be reinforced over time—either in follow-up sessions, weekly therapy sessions, and . . .

8. Support Groups

These support networks are crucial, especially when made up of teenage peers. Whether it's Narcotics Anonymous, Alcoholics

Anonymous, or school and community workshops, these groups continue to encourage, support, and reinforce abstinence as time goes on. Families, too, are encouraged to continue to help themselves, either by joining groups such as Al-Anon or by going into individual therapy themselves.

It's important to remember that a once-addicted teen is vulnerable to temptation. But with time, with the right support and help, and with positive results and changes, these teens will never go back on their self-destructive paths.

Drug addiction is a problem, but it has a cure. If parents learn to confront their kids without being defensive, if they learn to hear their teen's cry for help no matter how quiet its sound, and if they learn to see the signs of drug abuse without looking away, a problem can be stopped before it becomes a tragedy.

Hope—and help—is never far away. But drug abuse is only one crack in the mirror's reflection. Learning disabilities, juvenile delinquency, and physical and sexual abuse also add to depression's fuel. Let's go on to them now.

CHAPTER SIX:

Adding Insult to Injury: Learning Disabilities, Juvenile Delinquency, and Abuse

"What they wanted more than anything else was to be like 'regular kids.'"

—George Cadwalader

Words that don't make any sense. Attention that lasts only minutes at a time. Car thefts, fights in the schoolyard, and insensitivity to others. Voices that stutter. Bruises that are hidden in shame from the kids in class. . . .

Some teenagers never learn the three school "Rs." They are too weighed down with the three "Ds" of life: disability, delinquency, and dysfunctional family life. Physical or sexual abuse at home can lead to delinquency—and depression. A learning disability promotes a feeling of failure—and depression. Feelings of frustration can lead to acts of violence—and a depression with a life of its own.

One D is rarely seen without the other. And it's a rough combination to overcome. Imagine this scenario: You're 16 and already frustrated by your learning disability. There you are in Mr. MacDonald's English class, desperately trying to sink into your seat because you hadn't been able to read *Silas Marner* the night before—not because you didn't want to, but because you literally couldn't make sense of the words. Instead of being "good," you were "bad." You *are* bad. Isn't that what your

*from *Castaways: The Penikese Island Experiment*. By George Cadwalader. Chelsea, VT: Chelsea Green Publishing, 1988.

teachers are always saying: "Johnny could do better in school"? Isn't that how your parents feel? After all, they're always on your case about your failing grades and your supposedly high I.Q. It's a vicious cycle. The more you try, the more you fail. You're embarrassed and feeling guilty. Your self-esteem is nil. Maybe you turn to drugs as a way to feel better. Maybe you begin to act out—by breaking a window or joy-racing in a car instead of doing your homework. Sure, it's wrong, but who cares? At least you're doing *something*. At least you can feel in control. At least your sad, scared feelings are quiet for a while. . . .

This is a simplistic scenario, but the fact is that the three Ds play an important role in the many faces of adolescent depression. Delve slightly below the surface and chances are you will find that a depressed teen who has been acting out has a learning disability, or that he or she has been abused. Unfortunately, there's not enough space here to explore all three disorders in depth. But this chapter will help introduce you to the ins and outs of disability, delinquency, and dysfunctional families. It will help you see the signs and symptoms in your own teen. And it will guide you to treatments that really work. But most of all, these next few pages will offer hope—for the entire family.

LEARNING DISABILITIES AND YOUR TEENAGER

In today's world we hear the term "learning disabilities" more and more. In fact, 17 percent of all teenagers suffer from one of them. But what exactly is a learning disability? And how does it affect your child?

Actually, there are several types of learning disabilities, from speech impediments to reading problems. Teens can suffer from one disability or several at the same time. Their symptoms can range from mild to severe. Let's go over some of the major disabilities now.

1. Dyslexia.
Called a "Developmental Reading Disorder," this illness is marked by a high I.Q. combined with poor school performance.

It's usually revealed by the second grade, but sometimes kids don't show signs of dyslexia until they are in the fourth grade. Between 2 and 8 percent of school-age children have dyslexia, and it can be inherited. Dyslexic teens will omit, distort, or substitute words. They will have slow, halting reading skills and their reading comprehension is poor. Reading therapy is a must.

2. Math Blocks.

This usually crops up by the time a child is eight years old, and it's exactly what it implies: an inability to understand math and to recognize its symbols. Math block sufferers will have trouble copying figures correctly, understanding and memorizing multiplication tables, and counting.

3. Writing Disorders.

These teens will have difficulty composing paragraphs and writing their thoughts down on paper. Their compositions will have spelling and punctuation errors and poor organization. Writing disorders are usually seen in kids by the time they are seven, but less severe cases might not show up until they are ten or older. They, too, can be inherited.

4. Language Disorders.

Because language gets more and more complex with age, many language disorder cases are not discovered until a child has reached early adolescence. Here, teens have a limited vocabulary. They have difficulty learning new words, they speak in short sentences, and they might use unusual word orders when they talk. But the success rate for this disorder is good: by late adolescence many show great improvement, and between 3 and 10 percent of all sufferers are cured.

5. Speech Impediments.

Stuttering is the most noticeable of these disorders. Stutterers are three times more likely to be boys. They will have trouble pronouncing words in pressure-filled situations, but they are fine when singing, reciting, or talking to pets. Since stutterers usually try to avoid talking when they are feeling under stress, whether in a classroom, on the phone, or in a social setting, their school performance and their friendships suffer, as does their self-esteem. Ninety-eight percent of all cases begin before age ten, and the condition builds slowly over several months. Happily, 80 percent of all stutterers recover before they are sixteen, and 60 percent of these without any speech therapy at all.

Other speech impediments include lisps and difficulties in pronouncing *r, sh, th, f, z, l* and *ch* sounds. But with speech therapy, most of these kids can be cured.

More and more schools today are becoming savvy to the signs of learning disabilities. No longer is bad school performance punished out of hand. And with math tutoring and speech and reading therapy, learning disabilities can be successfully overcome.

FAMOUS FACES

Cher is as outspoken about her dyslexia as she is about her age and her career. She has spoken to reporters about the poor grades she received in school because she couldn't read. She thought something was wrong with her, that she was stupid—and the teachers concurred. Her dyslexia wasn't discovered until she was older, and she had already dropped out by then. But her disability did not hinder her remarkable success as an actress or singer. Perhaps if it had been discovered at an earlier age, her life would have taken a very different course. Dr. Cher, I presume?

But, before recovery, the scars of learning disability might already be in place. The fact is that *teens who suffer from learning disabilities associate learning with pain*. In a study of handicapped and healthy toddlers, Dr. Kay Donahue Jennings and colleagues discovered that handicapped kids don't try as hard to do a task because they just don't believe they will succeed. The moral? If you start defeated, you simply don't try. And if you don't try, you're not going to accomplish anything. It's a self-fulfilling prophecy that prompts teens to say: "See, I'm right. I'm a loser." And this leads to withdrawal, avoidance, poor grades . . . and depression.

In fact, conduct disorders and delinquency often have a

learning disorder at their root. A study done by Drs. Rob McGee and David L. Share found that if you treat the learning disability *instead* of the disruptive conduct, the bad behavior will disappear! And since one follows the other, let's now go on to. . . .

CONDUCT DISORDER AND DELINQUENCY

In his compelling book about an experimental "Outward Bound" program to help juvenile delinquents, *Castaways* author George Cadwalader describes a teen who, one moonlit night, systematically broke the legs of the chickens in the compound's backyard, one by one by one. . . .

This is a far cry from the Jets and the Sharks in *West Side Story,* but its violence speaks to all of us. Witness the popularity of William Golding's *Lord of the Flies,* which told of a group of upper-class boys who were stranded on a desert island and slowly became primitive, violent savages.

Some kids act out in groups, showing a great loyalty only to each other. Some kids, like the troubled youth who broke the chickens' legs, act out alone, methodically doling out their destruction in private. Still others act out only toward their parents at home. Conduct disorders range from minor scrapes and temper tantrums to hard-core delinquency. Let's go over the two main types of problem behavior:

1. Attention Deficit Hyperactivity Disorder (ADHD).

These teens have no attention span. They are impulsive and hyperactive, especially when attention is required at home and at school. ADHD victims can be fine when they are in a one-on-one situation, which makes it hard to diagnose in a doctor's office. ADHD teens show some or all of the following:

- Can't finish homework or get organized
- Won't listen
- Hands in messy, careless work
- Blurts out the answer before a teacher finishes asking the question
- Has trouble following directions

- Can't wait their turn
- Talks too much in class
- Twitches and fidgets in seat
- Runs around classroom
- Accident-prone at home
- Noisy
- Always ready to do something dangerous without thinking of the consequences, like roller skating down a steep hill
- Initiates self-destructive activities on the spur of the moment, like taking a ride in a fast car instead of doing homework.

ADHD kids are classic underachievers and six to nine times more likely to be boys than girls.

2. Conduct Disorders (CD).

These are the juvenile delinquents, the kids on the streets, the ones who violate the rights of others—at school, at home, and in the community. Their profile reads like a cliché—but it's real life.

CD kids commit petty crimes at an early age, going on to armed robberies and worse as they get older. They set fires and lie and cheat their way through school. They cut classes frequently and run away from home. Like the boy who broke the chickens' legs, they are cruel to animals and show little guilt or remorse for any of their actions. It's no surprise that CD victims do poorly in school. They are usually saddled with learning disabilities, ADHD tendencies, and abuse at home. Chances are their parents are alcoholics, too.

Psychiatrist Erik Erikson called these violent kids "pseudo-competent." Because of their underlying low self-esteem and feelings of helplessness and fear, they often turn to drugs for something to master and control. They also turn to gangs who agree that school achievement is for "wimps," and that real heroes take dangerous physical risks and fight with their fists. But drugs and gangs are not a part of the real, constructive world, and these teens are only faking their competency.

How do you treat a child with no conscience? Kids who have poor learning skills and who always expect criticism?

Programs like "Scared Straight" have gotten a lot of publicity. Unfortunately, they ultimately don't work. Followup studies showed that the results were only temporary, a Band-aid on a problem that was deeply imbedded in a delinquent's psyche. The fact is that you simply can't scare people into changing their behavior—especially defensive kids who feel omnipotent. "Yeah, well, you can end up in jail, but I won't," they say. Like a smoker who refuses to see the effects of cigarette smoke, these kids don't believe it will happen to them.

However, programs like "Scared Straight" can get their attention. And CD kids do need to be told of the dangers of their self-destructive path. But they need more. They need psychotherapy, family therapy, support, and sometimes medication. Like the victims of drug abuse we have seen in Chapter Five, CD kids need to get past their denial.

The therapeutic process is like a ride down a river filled with rapids. Support and understanding must be tempered with forcefulness and control. Good therapists will:

- Pick up where these CD kids have strengths—and almost force them to achieve in those areas. If a boy shows talent, say, in carpentry, he'll be encouraged to create more and actually start a business.
- Try to improve their weak areas, such as learning disabilities and basic knowledge. To teach his CD kids, George Cadwalader would "sneak" education into their daily routines. While they were doubling recipes and figuring out fractions on a tape measure, these kids never realized they were actually learning—and they didn't have to feel "stupid" or defensive in front of their peers.
- Stop CD victims from acting out by enforcing limits and controls—whether it be an island, as in the *Castaways* experiment, or a hospital with walls.
- Develop strong relationships with their CD patients. Like two-year-olds who idealize their parents, CD victims form

strong attachments to their therapists. But they will also become frightened of this tie, and they'll constantly put it to the test—with insults, theft, and acting out. A good therapist will say: "I still care about you, but stealing is totally unacceptable behavior." It cannot be dismissed.

EXPRESSIVE FACES

Juvenile delinquents and their gangs have been around for a long time. Whether it was the crowded, hot conditions at home, the long, hard working hours, or the promise of adventure, boys would take to the streets in droves in the late 1800s. In New York City alone, there were the Dead Rabbits, The Bowery Boys, The Little Plug Uglies, and the 40 Little Thieves. They were so disorderly that, according to the book, *Rites of Passage: Adolescents in America 1790 to the Present* (by Joseph Kett. New York: Basic Books, 1977), reformer Charles Loring Brace said: "The most dangerous classes of New York are its children!"

But ultimately the cure must come from these juvenile delinquents themselves. As George Cadwalader wrote in *Castaways*, "Letting the boy himself tell us by his own behavior whether or not he is salvageable may seem hard-hearted, but I can think of no other way to maximize the number we can save while protecting society from the ones we cannot."

PHYSICAL AND SEXUAL ABUSE

Dawn was only fourteen when she was raped by her girlfriend's father at a pajama party. No legal action was ever taken, but Dawn's pain had settled in to stay. She became rebellious. She slept too much. She lost twenty pounds. She lost interest in school and her outside activities. And she became sexually promiscuous.

Dawn's life was a shambles. She became pregnant and became a drug abuser and a runaway. Adding insult to injury, she also had learning disabilities that compounded her behavior.

Finally, when her parents told her of their plan to divorce, Dawn tried to kill herself. . . .

Perhaps if Dawn hadn't been sexually abused, nothing would have happened. Perhaps if the crime had come to light, she could have gone on with her life. But perhaps she still would have ended up in the same hopeless place. . . .

Whether the seed of bad behavior or merely another bad experience in a life filled with pain, abuse is ugly. The very people who could be helping its victims are taking advantage of them. Abused teenagers have to feel hopeless and helpless. Who can they trust? What's left? Drugs—and possibly suicide. . . .

Unfortunately, the problem becomes a family tradition. Teens who are abused usually become abusers themselves. Why? Because that's how they saw their parents act. That's how they saw their parents cope with the problems in their lives—by striking out with violence.

Abuse is also difficult to detect. Fear and guilt reign supreme, until, as in the case of a Long Island 16-year-old girl who had her sexually-abusing father killed, the rage boils over—or outside help is found.

Disability. Delinquency. Dysfunctional family life. These are the three Ds. Together, they build a wall of depression that must be noticed and understood before it can be broken down. But, as deadly as these are, the ultimate cry is yet to come. . . .

CHAPTER SEVEN

The Ultimate Cry: Suicide Today

"I hope never to become an adult."

—*Paul, 17*

• Billy was a prize student, a top-notch quarterback, and one of the most popular kids in class. Before he turned 16, he was already Student Council President and planning to go to Yale—just like his dad. His sixteenth birthday party was to be a gala affair, complete with catered food, live music, and over one hundred guests all gathered together on the family's back lawn. But the night before the party, Billy quietly went downstairs to his father's study. He took out the gun kept in the top desk drawer and shot himself. He left no note.

• "Dear Mom and Dad," fourteen-year-old Elizabeth wrote, "I'm sorry I have to do this, but I can't live any more. No one likes me, especially Craig. Please forgive me. Love, Lizzy." Elizabeth folded the note and placed it on her night table. She picked up her well-worn stuffed animal and put it next to her on the pillow. She then opened the bottle of tranquilizers her mother kept in the medicine cabinet and swallowed them all. Luckily, Elizabeth's parents came home before she died. But when she was 17, Elizabeth tried again. This time no one heard her cry for help.

• Sam started driving the family car before he was fourteen. When he was fifteen, he'd take it out when no one was home, pick up a couple of the guys and a couple of beers, and stay revved up and drunk all night long. When he was eighteen, Sam dropped out of vocational school and began to deal drugs.

Soon he had saved enough money from dealing to buy his own car. He couldn't wait to drive it around town the night he brought it home. But none of the guys were around. They were all at a school dance. Sam drove to the school and watched the kids going inside. Their laughter made him angry. He hit the steering wheel of his brand-new car and burned rubber as he sped away. Sam didn't need anyone. He decided to get drunk alone. At three o'clock that same morning, he decided to race an approaching train over the tracks. Sam lost.

The stories can go on, from teens with concerned parents, from teens with parents who couldn't care less, from delinquent kids in poor neighborhoods to kids with the best that money could buy.

Suicide. It happens to adolescents from all walks of life. It crosses all economic, social, and racial lines. It's the ultimate cry for help.

WHY SUICIDE?

Every year, two million children between fifteen and nineteen try to kill themselves—and every year some five thousand succeed. Some experts feel this is only the "tip of the iceberg," that the number of teens who commit suicide is actually four times the reported figure. This cry for help has reached such national proportions that June 1985 was officially made "Teenage Suicide Prevention Month," mobilizing educators, parents, teens, and community and corporate leaders to speak out and stop this tragic problem in its tracks.

Yes, these are hard, stressful times we live in. Though the past, too, had had its share of trouble (see Chapter One), today's teens perceive their world as "the worst of times." There's a lack of economic stability. Families are breaking up. Information bombards our youth on all sides, from TV ads that promise the world to headlines that scream violence, turbulence, and the threat of nuclear war. As I recently told *USA Today,* "There's less structure for teens today, what with working mothers, single parents, the available of drugs and the impersonal nature of modern life."

Adolescence has always been a time of experimentation, a time of trial and error—and a time when unhealthy habits, like drug-taking and alcohol consumption, can begin. Unfortunately, drug and alcohol abuse, delinquency, and crime have all risen over the years. And, as they increase, so do the suicide statistics.

But the drug and alcohol increases are not the sole instigators of suicide. A lack of communication. A splintering of family and life and its vital source of nourishment. Learning disabilities and conduct disorders. Isolation. Even trendiness. All enter into the equation. Listen to what this teenage girl told the NBC producer of the documentary *Dying for Attention:* "It's not trendy like blue jeans, but if I see so and so do it and it works for him, gets him the help he needs, things get better for him . . . well, then maybe I'll think about it for myself. . . ."

DEATH BY ANY OTHER NAME

Adolescents view life—and death—differently than adults. But, until recently, medical professionals treated teenage suicide with the same criteria they used for adults, which hindered clues to prevention and real communication. Understanding death is a process:

- Before they are a year old, children have no conception of death. To infants, absence translates into nonexistence.
- From one to five years, death is seen as something that can be changed, that can come and go.
- Between five and nine years of age, children personalize death, seeing it as a "wizard-like" being of night and darkness. It is the realm of magic and shadows, scary and distant.
- After nine, children understand what death means. But death is still seen as an external event in teens and young adults—something that will not happen to them for a long, long time. As the song in the hit movie *Fame* declared, "I'm gonna live forever!"

Because teens have such a different concept of death than adults, their suicide attempts are not as rooted in finality. When teens swallow too many pills, they are usually not thinking of that "black void," that point of no return. Instead, they might be trying to exert their independence by "running away." They might be angry at their parents and trying to punish them: "If I do this, they'll be sorry!" They might be angry at themselves, feeling a desperate need to punish themselves for real or imagined guilt. They might be emulating their parents, who harbor suicidal thoughts themselves. Or, after the death of someone close, teens might feel an uncontrollable urge to "join" their dead relative or friend because they miss him or her so much.

TO BE OR NOT TO BE

Why do some teens attempt suicide and others remain un-scathed? Suicide is a complex problem, and there is no one "type" of teen that heeds its deadly call. It's easy to recognize a *Rebel Without a Cause*-like teen hellbent on self-destruction. But what about the nice, quiet adolescent whose mind is churning around death as he eats his dinner? Or the well-respected, popular Type A teen who's crying out for help even as she studies for yet another exam?

GRIM STATISTICS

The following grim statistics come from the National Conference on Youth Suicide:

- Suicide is the third leading cause of death among teenagers in high school.
- Suicide is the Number Two cause of death among college students.
- For every teen who commits suicide, there are approximately 120 who try—and fail.
- Suicide is the leading cause of death among American Indian teenage boys.
- More black teens commit suicide in the North. More white teens kill themselves in the South.
- Ninety percent of the suicide attempts each year are committed by girls. Boys make up 70 percent of all successful suicides.

We have no crystal balls to help us see who will try to attempt suicide and who will not. We can't pigeonhole people into "suicide prototypes." But there are very definite symptoms of a teenager in trouble, signs that need a parent's attention before it is too late. Suicide is a harrowing possibility if your teen:

- Refuses to communicate with you
- Gives away a prized possession
- Becomes more and more morose and isolated
- Begins to show a lack of enthusiasm for school and a drop in grades
- Recently became heavily involved in drugs or alcohol
- Was a recent victim of an "accidental" overdose
- Had been a victim of child abuse
- Talks or displays a desire for revenge against you
- Overcomplains about aches and pains with no physical basis
- Makes self-loathing comments
- Has little energy
- Has just been rejected by a steady boy or girlfriend
- Has just moved to a new neighborhood or town
- Is in a household where one or both parents are depressed themselves
- Has suffered the loss of a parent, either through divorce, separation, or death
- Has overwhelming feelings of sadness and guilt
- Has frequent crying spells
- Is overly nervous and withdrawn
- Is exhibiting slow speech and action
- Suffers from insomnia—or sleeps too much
- Has a learning disorder that was misdiagnosed for many years
- Has a conduct disorder problem
- Lost too much weight—or gained too much too fast
- Has a sense of hopelessness for the future
- No longer sees any friends
- Talks about suicide and death
- Was close to someone who committed suicide

Remember, these symptoms alone do not necessarily mean your teen is contemplating suicide, but they do mean he or she is depressed and needs your help. Suicide is the final stop in the downward spiral of depression.

The more of these warning signs your youngster exhibits, the more you should be concerned—especially if your adolescent mentions or even just thinks suicidal thoughts.

Of all the faces of adolescent depression, suicide is the deadliest. It robs all of us of the future.

EXPRESSIONS

The best attack against suicide is knowledge. Armed with awareness, you can hear your teen's cry for help. Let's go over some of the particular characteristics of teenage suicide so you can better recognize its warning sounds.

1. The Battle Inside

Contrary to popular beliefs, suicide is not an alternative sought out by kids disgusted and impotent about nuclear war. Nor do teens see it as a "way out" because of the nihilistic rhymes they hear in heavy metal music (although these may resonate with the depression a youngster already feels). The reasons for suicide lie inside. It is the deadly result of the internal battle fought—and lost—by some teens who cannot cope with their conflicted feelings about family, love, school, and friends. It is psychological and social pressure—not current events—that trigger a teen's suicide attempt. However, one current event—the suicide of a well-known person or someone close to the adolescent—can trigger suicide.

FALSE FACES
MYTH: Youth suicide has reached epidemic proportions.

FACT: Wrong. In fact, though the suicide rates between 1956 and 1976 showed a 300 percent increase in suicide for boys and a 200 percent increase for girls, these numbers have dropped and leveled off in the 1980s. Why? Because the "baby boom" is over—and there are fewer

teens among us and more options open for them to
succeed. Yes, suicide is still prevalent among such cultures
as Native American Indians and Canadians, but taken as a
whole, the suicide rate for teens is much lower than for
our solitary, isolated middle-aged and elderly citizens.

2. Girls and Boys Together

Girls attempt suicide more often than boys, but boys who
attempt suicide are more likely to succeed. Why? The answer
lies in their personalities. As we have seen in Part I, boys don't
discuss their feelings as much as girls do. They are more
action-oriented and tend to do things with their friends instead
of talk. Some boys keep their feelings so bottled up that when
they resort to suicide, it's with a dangerous mindset of finality.
Girls, on the other hand, take a more romantic view of suicide.
In fact, many girls who "flirt" with suicide do so because they've
been rejected by a boyfriend. Rejection by a friend whom they
have become dependent upon transfers to their parents, who
are seen as having rejected them as well.

3. An Impulsive Streak

By their very nature, teens are impulsive, and they will
plunge into something without ever "seeing the forest for the
trees." Unfortunately, this impulsive trait can carry over into
suicide. Combined with a teen's more external view of death,
this impulsiveness can be deadly. A teen suicide can be triggered
by what adults might feel is a small problem—a failure in school
or a snub by a friend. As parents, we must be aware of the fact
that what looks insignificant to us with our more adult perspective can be overwhelming to an impulsive teen.

4. Lethal Weapons

Ease, accessibility, and reaction time are all factors in the way
a suicidal teen might choose to die. An overdose of antidepressants is the most common form of teenage suicide because it is
so accessible, but it is also a method that can be caught in time.

Like Anna Karenina, many suicidal teens will jump in front of
a train—an accessible but irrevocable cry for help. This year
alone, New Jersey railroad engineers have witnessed at least ten

teenagers who have killed themselves by jumping onto the tracks as a fast train approached.

Carbon monoxide poisoning is another accessible lethal weapon. When the English government switched from the more dangerous "coal gas" to the less toxic natural gas, suicide rates went down. It was no longer as easy to die.

5. Masked Murderer

Last year, *The New York Times* reported the sad story of a young teenage girl who was so taken with the movie *Stand By Me* that she tried to race a train just as the boys in the film had. She was killed.

Many "accidental" deaths are really suicide. Motorcycle crashes, auto accidents, refusals to take medicine, drug overdoses, dangerous lifestyles—all could be considered disguised suicide attempts.

6. The Chemical Connection

Suicidal teens show a decrease in the brain's chemical messenger serotonin and in growth hormone secretions. *The New York Times* recently wrote about a study done at the University of Pittsburgh from 1980 to 1987. There, Drs. Neal D. Ryan and Joanquim Puig-Antich analyzed the growth hormone secretions of 140 boys and girls between twelve and eighteen years of age. Of those 140 teens, 34 had deficiencies of growth hormone secretions in their brain. These 34 were also seriously depressed and had tried to commit suicide.

7. The Family Tie

Families are powerful. We have seen how their positive, nurturing influences can help teens grow, and how their pull in resisting change and denying depression can hurt. If one or both parents are depressed, there's a good chance their sons or daughters will be, too. If one or both parents are suicidal or have committed suicide themselves, the risk of their sons or daughters thinking along the same lines are high. They might want to join their parents "on the other side." They might believe that if it was good enough for their parents, why not them? They might feel so much rage and self-inflicted blame that they see no other way out but death. In fact, a suicide in the family increases the risk for teens six times.

8. Drug Talk

Substance abuse is a problem, but it is not the cause of suicide. Teens use drugs to help them cope with an underlying depression. But, as I've discussed in Chapter Five, drugs can make a depression worse. Family lives are disrupted. School grades fall. Friends drop away. Serious legal trouble can mount. Difficult life experiences—a move, a divorce, or a death—are even more traumatic.

And when the drugs fail—and they ultimately always do—addicted teens are left with a tremendous sense of loss. Even their drugs have failed. Their depression hits bottom, and there is no way out but one: suicide.

FAMOUS FACES

Sid Vicious and his girlfriend/manager Nancy were at the forefront of the punk rock movement—both in London and in the United States. Unfortunately for these two young adults, they lived what they sang. Hell-bent on self-destruction, they became heroin addicts, with a costly daily habit they could not kick. Sid's group split up. Broke and disillusioned, he and Nancy moved to Manhattan's Chelsea Hotel, home of avant-garde artists, musicians, actors, and writers. At the Chelsea, their habit and their self-esteem continued to spiral down, deeper and deeper, until one night, when they were both in a drug-induced haze, Nancy begged Sid to kill her. He complied, slashing her with a knife. The next morning, they woke up and the bed was soaked in blood. Nancy stumbled into the bathroom and died. Not long afterward, Sid died of an overdose—before his trial for murder was to begin.

---

8. Type A Teens and Suicide

The Student Council President who kills himself. The Harvard-bound science whiz who swallows too many pills. When Type A teens commit suicide, they leave shock and surprise in their wake. No one ever expects these popular, successful, attractive people to kill themselves, let alone be depressed. In fact, only 4 percent of these Type A teens attempt suicide—*but 30 percent seriously contemplate it.* Why? Possibly because they equate failing in school with failing their parents. They desperately need constant and continuous approval from others—an impossible goal to maintain. As we have seen in Chapter Three, these teens paint themselves in a corner over and over again. They are indeed their own worst enemy.

9. *College Break*

Suicide is the leading cause of death in college. Ten thousand college kids a year attempt suicide, and between 500 and 1000 are successful. Think about it: Not only do college students have to deal with the normal adolescent conflicts they faced in high school, but suddenly they are thrust into a strange, new world of fierce competition and culture shock. Homesickness, loneliness, academic pressure, and career anxiety abound in college, leading some young adults down the road to depression . . . and suicide.

10. *Risky Business*

Where there is a will, there is, unfortunately, a way. How much does a teenager want to die? In my years as an adolescent psychiatrist, I have found the answer to this question crucial for successful treatment—as well as one of the greatest indicators of risk.

It's a question that must be posed to the teens themselves, because parents grossly underestimate their children's wish to die. In a study of 752 families with teenagers who had attempted suicide, it was found that mothers were unaware of how deeply their kids' suicidal thoughts ran—even after the suicide attempt!

Even though a teen's desire to die is a high risk factor, it's not the only motivating force. Other predictors include:

- Degree of hopelessness
- History of suicide in the family
- History of previous attempts
- Social isolation and a lack of a good support network
- History of recent loss or separation, including death, divorce, a move, or a graduation
- Heavy drug use

These predictors are not etched in stone. Just because a teen is burdened with one or more of these high risk factors does not mean that suicide is a *fait accompli*. But almost every teen who *does* attempt suicide will have one or more of these predictors in his or her background. In my study at the Psychiatric Institute of Montgomery County of thirteen teens with drug problems who attempted drug-involved suicide, I discovered that eleven of them had at least one alcoholic parent. Six suffered from a separation or divorce within the past two years. Three had a history of suicide in their family. Five had recently moved. Five had a learning disability. Four had suffered from physical or sexual abuse. In fact, only two out of the thirteen teens lived with their original mothers and fathers and had no family conflicts.

11. Clusters

On February 4, 1984, in Westchester County, New York, a 13-year-old boy committed suicide by hanging himself. On February 14, another boy, a year older, joined him. On February 16, a 19-year-old boy shot himself. On February 21, a 17-year-old boy hung himself. On February 24, another 19-year-old boy hung himself. In only three weeks, five teens in the same community killed themselves.

In 1987, four teenagers in Bergenfield, New Jersey committed suicide. Six days later, four other teens in a Chicago suburb had followed suit.

These rampant suicides are called clusters—a phenomenon in which one suicide triggers more. Only about 5 percent of all teenage suicides a year are considered cluster cases, but because of their "advance notice" they can be better prevented than isolated suicides. The Centers for Disease Control in Atlanta suggests that communities can best stop cluster suicides by:

- Formulating a community action plan now, before a suicide cluster begins and panic sets in
- Avoiding sensationalism
- Identifying those teens with high risk factors and offering them counseling services

- Altering those places or situations that might cause clustering, such as blocking off a park where suicide attempts are taking place.

In addition to these guidelines, educators, parents, and community leaders must encourage teens to discuss their feelings on suicide both in the classroom and at home.

There is one crucial difference between those teens that try to kill themselves and those that never do: *they see suicide as a solution—not the problem it really is*.

When teenagers attempt suicide, it's not the act of death they want. They want relief from an intolerable situation and from intolerable pain. They are crying for help.

It is up to us—parents, other teens, teachers, and members of the community—to recognize that cry.

At the National Conference on Youth Suicide this past June, psychologist Peter Alsop said, "How do you eat an elephant? One bite at a time." Recognizing the cry for help is the first bite. Implementing programs at school and on the community level is another. Fighting our own fears as parents and offering real help is a third.

Slowly, we can change things. Slowly, we can give our teens the future they deserve.

Like Pandora and her mythical box, we have glimpsed into the mirror and have seen the demons unleashed. But there is one more face to examine: hope.

Let's now go on to the treatment and prevention of adolescent depression.

PART III

Positive Reflections: Treatments and Cures

CHAPTER EIGHT
Treatment That Works

"He isn't a bad shrink. You can't fool him."

—*Patti, 15*

I remember when Craig, an eighteen-year-old college student, first came to see me. He had recently informed his parents that he would not be going back to school, despite their arguments, tears, and protests. When his father asked Craig to see a therapist—just once—to discuss his decision, Craig readily agreed. He saw it as an opportunity to prove to his parents that his decision was sane—and right.

Craig sat in the chair opposite mine, seemingly confident and willing to talk. He good-naturedly spoke about his "up-tight" parents and he calmly described the competition at school and how it didn't fit in with his philosophy of living for today, of enjoying life now.

Near the end of the first session, I mentioned that it seemed Craig was describing a story about a friend, someone he knew, instead of himself. It was odd that he could treat such a momentous decision with such calmness, that the strong feelings that should have gone along with his decision were absent.

Craig looked thoughtful, and he didn't reply. But the next day, he called for another appointment. He hadn't slept well and he'd been thinking over what I had said.

During the next session, Craig was more open. He tentatively talked about his feelings of competition with his father, and our sessions became a weekly routine. Further down the road he began to see his internal problems with success and his real reasons for leaving college. . . .

A few months later, Craig had decided to go back to school, and he graduated last year with honors.

Craig was able to work through his problems with an individual therapist. But another teen might require medication to combat his or her anxiety. Still another teen might benefit from group therapy and skill training. And a severely depressed teen with suicidal tendencies would need hospitalization and 24-hour care.

Therapy is a unique process. Though there are certain guidelines and specific treatments that have been proven to succeed, not every method is right for every depressed teen. And, in most cases, treatments must be combined for maximum results.

Before we go on to specific treatments, take a few moments to look over these statements. They will help you define your own teen's depression. Remember, individual teens are much more complex than these generalizations, and accurate diagnosis can only come from a doctor who can evaluate and determine first-hand the illness and the cure.

YOUR TEEN MIGHT BE SUFFERING FROM A SITUATIONAL DEPRESSION IF:

1. You have recently moved.
2. You have recently gone through a divorce or a separation.
3. You're just moved to a new town.
4. He has just graduated from high school.
5. She has just started college in another state.
6. He has broken up with his girlfriend.
7. She has had a fight with her friends.
8. He has just been passed over for Student Council president.
9. She's just failed a test.
10. A recent loss, separation, or move has sent him into despair.
11. A recent loss, separation, or move has changed her.
12. Right after his rejection, he started taking drugs.
13. Right after she got a C, she became withdrawn and dropped her friends.
14. Prior to the loss, separation, or move he had shown no evidence of depression or anxiety.

RX:

Teens suffering from situational depression do not always need therapy. Healthy teens don't want to stay depressed, nor do they want to foster the dependent, "babyish" feelings that go along with their pain. The want their sad feelings to go away fast. If they have a relationship with a concerned and accessible adult figure—a parent, a relative, a teacher, or a religious leader—they can sometimes work out their problems on their own. But if their depression lasts longer than two weeks, outside help must be sought.

YOUR TEEN MIGHT BE SUFFERING FROM A CHRONIC, NEUROTIC DEPRESSION IF:

1. You are depressed yourself.
2. He constantly puts himself down.
3. She constantly puts the world around her down.
4. He is pessimistic about life.
5. She feels out of control.
6. He has been withdrawn and depressed for a long time.
7. There is little communication between you.
8. She expresses feelings of hopelessness.
9. He expresses feelings of helplessness.
10. She worries a lot about her health.
11. He always believes the worst will happen.
12. She never lasts long with self-improvement plans.
13. His self-esteem is nil.
14. She has a learning disability.
15. His school grades are poor.
16. She has few friends.
17. He never goes out on dates.
18. She thinks about suicide.

RX:

Teens who are chronically depressed need long-term treatment. Their negative feelings stick to their souls like iron to a magnet. Therapy must focus on the positive through individual therapy with a doctor who:

- Consistently and logically keeps reminding them of the successes they always choose to ignore
- Supports them and offers security.
- Helps them resolve their underlying conflicts so that they can deal with their feelings better.
- Helps them challenge the hidden assumptions about themselves and life which are both untrue and depressing.

Because these teens cling to their depression like a lifeboat, individual therapy is a long, involved process. But combined with family therapy, group support, and skill training, many chronic depressed teens learn that their lifeboat was full of holes—and that there is a better, more hopeful way to live.

YOUR TEENAGER MIGHT BE SUFFERING FROM A MAJOR AFFECTIVE DISORDER IF:

1. There is a history of unipolar or bipolar depression in the family.
2. He has extreme mood swings.
3. She has hallucinations.
4. He is violent and dangerously lashes out for no reason.
5. Her sense of reality is way off base.
6. He cannot function in school or at home.
7. She has wildly unrealistic feelings of guilt and self-reproach.
8. He shows major changes in sleeping or eating patterns.

RX:

Since major affective disorders can be biologically based, medications work well to keep highs and lows and depressive episodes in check. Individual therapy focuses on support as well as helping these teens accept the fact that they have a major illness. Skill training teaches them ways to cope better with their disabilities and with other people, which, in turn, enhances their self-esteem and confidence. Practical advice and education is crucial. A positive entry into the real world—a new job, new friends, new interests—can do much more for disturbed teens than a deep exploration into their souls.

THE MANY FACES OF TREATMENT

Will Rogers once said, "Even if you're on the right track, you'll get run over if you just sit there." Knowing your child is depressed is not enough. And all the best intentions in the world can't always stop a depression that's taken root. Sometimes getting outside help is not only a necessary step but a crucial one.

Let's briefly go over the different treatments available today and see how they work—and why.

1. "Do you want to talk about it?", or, Psychotherapy

Therapists are not magicians. When a depressed teen walks through their door, they can't wave a magic wand or look into a crystal ball and make things better immediately. Psychotherapy is a process, one that can be rewarding for both you and your teen. But it does takes time:

Time to Build Up a Relationship....

A good relationship between patient and therapist is paramount. But it is a fragile one. On one hand, the therapist must instill trust—in teens who have learned never to trust a soul. This can only happen over time, as the therapist consistently implies, "I will be here. I will listen."

On the other hand, therapists can never make up for a teen's early deprivations, nor can they imply that they can make the teen happy. Ultimately, like everyone else, the therapist too would fall short—and the teen will never feel that happiness is ever possible. A therapist must always convey, "I don't give everything. I can't give everything. Fortunately, you don't need that—though it might feel like you do. In any case I *am* here."

IF A TEEN HAS ATTEMPTED SUICIDE, A THERAPIST MUST:

Use reason....

to show the teen that this is a temporary state of mind and that the problems he or she faces can be solved—with the right kind of help.

Force Home . . . .
   these facts because a depressed teen feels that nothing
will help.
Appeal to Moral Issues . . . .
   that include society taboos and the tragic impact on the
teen's family if his or her suicide succeeds.
Intrude . . . .
   on the teen's life by any means that work, including a
signed contract that the teen will not try suicide unless he
or she speaks to the therapist first.
Mobilize . . . .
   the family so that all potentially dangerous weapons are
out of the house.
Hospitalize . . . .
   the teen if necessary for 24-hour supervision until the
crisis has passed.

Like an English-speaking guide in a foreign country, the
therapist can point out the places to explore and provide
explanations. But even after the teen trusts the guide and
borrows some courage, the guide can only lead so far. The actual
appreciating, internalizing, and growing is ultimately an experience one must do alone. If teens become too dependent on
their "guide," they will never see for themselves what vistas are
out there to explore.

Time to Get Involved. . . .
During his past eighteen months in therapy, Carl had been
making steady progress. A learning-disabled teen with a chronic
depression, he had slowly begun to gain a confidence about
himself. He had a group of new friends; he joined the soccer
team at school; he did his remedial exercises and his homework
with care. But he still had problems getting to school on
time—no matter how many alarm clocks he set, no matter how
much his parents screamed and cajoled, no matter how he
prepared himself the night before. His therapist, determined to
get Carl over this last hurdle, went to his house every morning

and literally dragged him off to school. Within two weeks, Carl was in school, on his own, by the time the last bell had rung.

This scenario might seem extreme, but it shows that an adolescent therapist has to get involved, and that the type and degree of involvement is as individual as the therapeutic relationship itself. Of course, temporary "real" help of this kind should be rare to avoid encouraging too much dependence on a guide who is carrying too much of the load.

Time to Develop and Grow. . . .

Therapy centers on growth, in order to better understand, appreciate, and participate in life.

For Type A teens, the process emphasizes their problems with success. A good therapist will help them:

- Separate achievement failure from real loss. (No one dies if you get a C; it just feels that way.)
- Internalize their achievements, to see them as a natural outgrowth of their talents and abilities instead of a demanded price for love.
- Define excellence and slowly realize that no one's perfect and no one always wins . . . not even them.

One of my patients a few years back, a Type A 16-year-old boy, had been seeing a counselor for several months before beginning his sessions with me. His previous counselor had unwittingly angered the teen. The boy lashed out so strongly that the counselor was angered and defeated, and the therapeutic process came to a dead halt. But that counselor had missed a valuable opportunity. If she had said, "You might be disappointed in me, but come on, you're not devastated, this wasn't a life or death situation," the teen might have gained some valuable insights on his reactions, and why perfection was so important to him. In addition, the therapist's ability to tolerate the teen's anger without loss of self-esteem or counterattack would have been a powerful object lesson.

THE SIX THINGS EVERY TEENAGER NEEDS

1. Love.

Freud once said that the capacity to give and receive love was an important key to mental health. Without a parent's love, a teen cannot develop a sense of trust, self-worth, or confidence.

2. Space.

Teens need room to grow, to think, to learn—and to make mistakes. Overly protective and overly involved parenting does not foster independence and the confidence that comes from flying solo.

3. Friends.

They help in the transition from home to the outside world, offering comfort, safety, and empathy.

4. Traditions.

Whether it be religion, ethnic ties, rites of passage celebrations, or family trees, traditions give a teen roots—and a way to define the present.

5. Limits.

Every teen needs boundaries to learn to function in the real world. Rules provide a base, and a security. Even if a teen ultimately rebels against the rules set down, he or she will know what it is they are fighting.

6. Adults.

From parents to teachers, community and religious leaders to favorite relatives, teens need to know there is someone older to talk to when things get rough, a role model who is accessible, understanding, and wise.*

(Adapted from "Myths and Needs of Contemporary Youth" by Saul V. Levine in *Adolescent Psychiatry: Developmental and Clinical Studies, Volume 14*. Chicago: The University of Chicago Press. 1987.)

For situationally depressed teens, therapy can be more traditional, where insights about past behavior will bring an understanding, an acceptance and a developmental leap forward: "Okay, that's settled, now on with life."

But chronically depressed "nay-sayers" can't benefit from insight-oriented therapy—at least at the beginning. Their depression is the only identity they have. They have no interest in their past or their future. Their feelings of hopelessness and helplessness have permeated every aspect of their lives. As Dr. K.M. Tooley once said, "The symptomatic depression... is based not on self-hatred or guilt, but seems instead to be deficiency disease, a lack of love for their lives and a lack of hope (or even thought) that they might feel quite differently in a year or two."

In order for the therapeutic process to work, a good therapist will involve "nay-sayers" with the therapist and use their interest in the therapist to help them become involved with themselves.

This is easier said than done. Because of their hopeless and helpless attitudes, "nay-sayers" have difficulty viewing their own behavior. They have no defenses to withstand anxiety. They have no role models or idealized memories to help them through a rough time.

And they expect the therapist to be as demanding, as critical, and as disapproving as the other people in their lives.

How does a therapist get beyond this wall? Through:

- Caring support
- Consistency in attitude, routine, and structure
- A firm logic that points out success as it occurs.

But as these "nay-sayers" begin to view their therapist as an ally, they can become overly dependent. Like a prisoner who has been unexpectedly set free, they begin to increase their expectations for themselves—and what the therapist can deliver. Nobody can grab the moon, and they are bound to be disappointed once again. These teens might become whiny, angry, or sullen—"testing" the therapist to see if he or she really cares. They might revert to the comfort and safety of their "old familiar friend" depression and drop out of therapy before they are cured.

The only way to overcome this is for the therapist to remain consistent and to clarify the fact that "I am not everything. I don't pretend to be. But I am here to listen. I care..."

As these chronically depressed teens develop relationships outside of therapy, more traditional insight therapy can begin. A good therapist will "shift gears," changing from an unqualified friend to a guide. Through this later therapeutic process, these teens will learn about the ambivalence of life. They will bring their feelings of love closer to their feelings of hate, their happy experiences more closely linked to their frustrating times.

By understanding ambivalence, these teens have a chance to grow. They get to see, first-hand, how their depression served as an avoidance of life, and how their fears of loss and rejection contaminated and distorted all their relationships.

A slow process? Yes. But healthy attitudes, like all good things in life, need time to grow.

2. Medicines of the Mind, or, Pharmaceuticals

Their names will never appear in a classroom spelling bee. They probably won't crop up in a high school homework assignment. But in the past three decades, pharmaceutical drugs have changed the outlook on psychology for good.

Difficult to pronounce and hard to remember, these antidepressants have provided a vital link between mind and body, a proven way to bring the chemicals of the brain into better balance and alter moods. Sciences like biopsychiatry and psychopharmacology have created safer, more predicable ways of correcting biologically based depressions than psychotherapy alone.

Because these antidepressants are the number-one agent of suicide in teens, they must be administered carefully. And they must never be the sole method of treatment. Because of the unique psychology of adolescents (see Chapter One), depressed adolescents suffer more from outside trauma that their adult counterparts, and consequently antidepressants don't work as well.

But drug therapy, in conjunction with other therapies, can successfully treat major affective disorders in teens. Here is a brief listing of the more common antidepressants used—*under a doctor's close supervision:*

Tricyclic Antidepressants (TCAs).

Named for their three-ring molecular structure, these drugs increase the level of the brain's neurotransmitters—the chemical messengers that regulate our emotions. They have a success rate of between 60 and 85 percent and are always tried first.

Side effects can include: blurry vision, dry mouth, sleepiness, constipation, and rapid pulse.

Brand names*: Elavil, Pamelor, Norpramin, Tofranil, Imipramine, Desyrel.

If TCAs don't work, the psychiatrist may consider prescribing:

MAO Inhibitors.

These block an enzyme called monamine oxidase (MAO), which breaks down those chemical neurotransmitters in the brain. When MAO inhibitors are used, patients must avoid alcohol, cheese, and over-the-counter medications for colds, coughs, flus, and hay fever. *Always check with your doctor or pharmacist for a complete list of medications and foods that must be avoided while taking this drug.*

Side effects can include: high blood pressure, headaches, vomiting, irregular pulse, nausea, stiff neck, and light sensitivity.

Brand names: Nardil, Parnate, Marplan.

For bipolar depressions, the drug of choice is:

Lithium Carbonate.

This is a natural mineral salt that is used to stabilize extreme highs and lows in manic-depressive disorders. Lithium prevents manic episodes from recurring in 70 percent of all cases, and it softens the intensity of the subsequent lows. *Correct dosage is essential and the drug must be taken under close medical supervision with careful monitoring of blood levels.*

Side effects can include: sleepiness, confusion, tremor, headaches, nausea, diarrhea, restlessness, rashes, and hallucinations.

*NOTE: The brand names listed throughout this section do not constitute a complete list, but simply reflect some of the more common medications that may be used to treat depression.

These side effects are usually dose-related. There is also some concern about lithium's long term effect on the kidneys. Patients should discuss this risk with their psychiatrist, since it is not clear that this is actually a side effect.

Brand names: Lithium, Eskalith, Lithane, Lithobid

If lithium doesn't work, the psychiatrist may try:

Carbamazepine.

Chemically, this drug is related to the TCA imipramine. An anticonvulsant, for a long time it was used solely to treat epilepsy. Today, it is used for manic-depression either in combination with lithium or alone. Carbamazepine has a 50 percent success rate when other drug treatments have failed. *It must be monitored very closely because of its potentially harmful side effects.*

Side effects can include: drowsiness and irritability. Most important, there have been reported cases of suppression of blood-cell production. A careful physical exam, including a full laboratory study of the blood cells, should precede use.

Brand name: Tegretol.

These drugs have been proven to help depression, but they all take time to work. Usually they begin to take effect in seven to ten days, but in some cases, between four to six weeks can go by before results are seen—an interminable time for impatient adolescents. Many severely depressed teens will begin to think that the drugs won't do anything. They can start to distrust their doctor and fall deeper and deeper into despair. That's why antidepressants are only given for major illnesses in teens, and they must always be used in conjunction with other therapy. If the depression is severe, or if there is any threat of suicide, it is safe to begin drug treatment in the hospital.

3. It's All in the Family, or, Family Therapy

Love can go far within the family circle. But when a teenager is depressed, other needs, other feelings, come into play. We have seen the power of the family tie and its need to keep change at bay at all costs. But denial is only one part of the problem. Families, too, need therapy because:

- Chances are, their teen's depression has caused a lot of family tension. From unhappiness to marital discord, a parent's problems and stress must also be treated.

- The parents might themselves be abusing drugs, considering suicide, or depressed.

- Their own problems and prejudices might cause parents to reject therapy and sabotage their teen's treatment.

- Once a teen enters therapy and starts feeling better, the family balance will be threatened. Then parents will need skillful counseling to avoid accidentally interfering with continued improvement.

MIRROR IMAGE: ARE YOU DEPRESSED TOO?

If your adolescent is chronically depressed, it's possible that you are, too. If any of these statements ring true, it might be wise to seek outside help for yourself. Parents who are depressed can pass their pain on to their children—and hinder a successful treatment program.

1. I have insomnia—or I sleep my days away.
2. I've lost weight—or gained too much.
3. The simplest errands are too much of a chore.
4. Life is grey.
5. I hate the way I look.
6. I can't do anything right.
7. All I want to do is lie around and watch TV all day.
8. I don't want to see my friends.
9. I have no sex drive.
10. I have crying spells for no reason.
11. I worry excessively about my health.
12. Sometimes life doesn't seem worth living.
13. I stopped taking showers and taking care of myself.
14. Everybody's against me.
15. Nobody understands me. I'm all alone.

4. The Power of Support, or, Group Therapy and Support Groups

Jason, a 14-year-old, had been a member of one of my groups for several weeks. During that time, he refused to be quiet and listen to the others. He kept making jokes and circumventing any serious discussions we were trying to have. His attitude was starting to upset the other teens, so in the next session, I suggested a psychological exercise. The kids would take turns picking someone in the group to lead them around the room while they were blindfolded. When it was his turn, Jason reluctantly put on his blindfold, but he refused to pick anyone. He was silent. I commented that he looked scared. Jason mumbled, "No one wants me to pick them. They all hate me." Suddenly, the group saw a new side of Jason—a scared boy who didn't trust anyone but me. The other group members were able to be more sympathetic to his plight and help him overcome his fear of teens his own age.

There is power in numbers. A group can reinforce and strengthen the insights gained in individual therapy. In Chapter Five, we saw the importance of peer group therapy for drug-dependent teens. For families that are hesitant to start individual therapy themselves, multifamily therapy is also a good alternative. Here, older families can provide a hopeful, more positive model for newcomers. They can calm and support shakier members, and they can guide new families through the therapy process with more empathy and tact.

Support groups, too, are important—especially for long-term results. One look at the yellow pages and the countless organizations available for help leap out: Alcoholics Anonymous, Narcotics Anonymous, Tough Love, groups for depressed families, suicide survivors, parents of learning-disabled children . . . the list goes on. If none of the groups are available in your area, contact your state mental health association for information about the closest resources.

Your therapist, local hospitals, schools, and community centers can all guide you to the right groups for continuous support outside of the therapy office.

5. Action Speaks Louder Than Words, or, Behavioral Therapy and Skill Training

Stimulus/response. To behavioral therapists, the way to change a depressed feeling is to change the stimulus/response connection. If a teenage girl's extra weight is adding fuel to her depression, getting rid of the fattening foods in the house will stop her from snacking when she comes home from school. If a learning-disabled boy hates his school because he can't keep up, changing his environment so that he's with other learning-disabled kids can stop his sense of failure; he can actually start enjoying himself.

Cognitive therapy, a short-term behavior-based program, deals with the thought process that goes on when a stimulus creates a certain response. A cognitive therapist will work with both parents and teens to change negative thoughts logically and rationally—and, consequently, change negative responses. He or she will use written assignments, charts, and role-playing to help patients see where their negative beliefs come into play. Here's an example, derived from an article by T. C. R. Wilkes and A. John Rush ("Adaptations of Cognitive Therapy for Depressed Adolescents," *Journal of the American Academy of Child and Adolescent Psychiatry*, v27, n3. May 1988)

Chris was a depressed 15-year-old with dyslexia. His mother, a concerned and loving parent, worried about him constantly. When both Chris and his mother recorded their feelings for one week, it was discovered that at the times his mother fretted most, Chris was actually feeling fine—watching television or doing his homework without angst.

Another example derived from the above article involves Tina, a Type A teen, and her cognitive therapist in a role play. The therapist is playing a baiting, insensitive school chum:

THERAPIST: You're no good, Tina.

TINA: What do you mean?

THERAPIST: You didn't win a prize.

TINA: Not everybody can win a prize. Besides, I came in second.

THERAPIST: That's no good, you've been second before. It's no good unless you win.

TINA: I still enjoy being with my friends and a teacher has to award people's efforts as well. Just because you don't win doesn't mean that you are no good.

THERAPIST: Okay, you've convinced me.

By acting out a more rational response to a competitive situation that would normally have devastated her, Tina saw first-hand the reality her Type A behavior never let her see.

Other skill training includes remedial reading, math, or learning-disability exercises to further enhance a teen's confidence that he or she can cope—and succeed.

6. When a Therapy Visit isn't Enough, or, Hospitalization

Attempted suicide. Drug addiction. Overdose. Abusive violence. When teens are in danger of hurting themselves or others, the security and safety of a hospital is crucial.

Visits of two weeks to one month are needed for acute emergency situations. Detoxification, intense suicidal tendencies, and severe bipolar depressions that need time for medication to work—all benefit from crisis intervention. The concentration of drug therapy and support in a contained hospital setting stops a tragic disaster and speeds recovery. Usually, individual therapy begins as well, which is continued on an outpatient basis after the teen is discharged.

Teens with more severe depressive illnesses and chemical addiction need longer hospital stays—anywhere from two months to four months. Here, as we have seen in Chapter Five, individual, family, and peer group therapy all play important and integrated roles.

The few teens who suffer from psychosis and severe mental illness have a tremendous amount to overcome and learn. Their hospital stay must be more long-term, calculated in years instead of months.

THE THERAPY PROGRAM

All these therapies work together. Individual therapy works best with pharmaceuticals in major affective disorders. A combination of family therapy, individual therapy and skill training might work best for a "nay-sayer." A combination of all six might be necessary for a suicidal or drug-addicted teen.

To determine the best program to follow, an initial evaluation is necessary. Here are some of the questions I use to evaluate my new patients—and to determine which treatments will probably have the most success:

1. Does the teen have any organic problem or physical illness?

We do differential diagnoses on every teen who comes to the Psychiatric Institute of Montgomery County. Here, various tests show us if a teen is suffering from a physical ailment that can cause his or her depression. We also determine if there are any learning disabilities, conduct disorders, or attention deficit disorders that must also be addressed.

2. What is the teen's psychological history?

A complete background history is taken, to help determine the teen's psychological development.

3. Why is the teen here?

Addressing the situation that brought a teen in to see me is as important as the underlying depression to help discover the best therapeutic approach.

4. Is the teen motivated to get well?

Understanding the answer to this question helps me see if I should use a more classic, insight-related therapy or a program best suited for a chronically neurotic depressed teen.

5. Will the teen's family be supportive?

Teens need their family's support for optimum growth. If a family is resistant to the therapy program, I must find out why—and discuss it with them.

Outside help is crucial. But there is much we, as parents, can do for our teens at home. Let's go on to the ways parents can help—starting right now.

CHAPTER NINE
Parents Can Help

"The value of a two-parent system? That's easy. One night, it's 'I hate you, Daddy!' The next night, it's 'I hate you, Mommy!'"

—Parent of a teenager

Picture it: There you are, the parent of an adorable, sweet-tempered child, a boy or girl who listens to you, who shows you affection, who looks up to you. . . . A child you know as well as yourself. Then, slowly, almost imperceptibly, the "Big A" strikes. Your child becomes The Adolescent. Suddenly, there's a stranger in the house—complete with loud music, messy rooms, and unpredictable behavior.

Welcome to the world of the teenage years.

The relationship between parents and teens has sold more articles, created more movie scripts, and kept TV hopping more than any other subject. It's universal, timeless, and perpetually perplexing to parents. But as confused and estranged as you might feel, it's important to remember that there is also no more intense a tie than the one between parent and teen. Here's proof: A recent article in *The Washington Post* reported a survey done among American teens to determine their chief concerns. The number-one top worry was the death of a parent—even above the threat of nuclear war!

Clearly your influence can go far, and as parents, the support you give your teen can have more impact than you might think.

HOW WELL DO YOU HANDLE YOUR TEENAGER'S DEPRESSION?

Maybe you believe you're doing everything possible. Maybe you can't figure out any other ways of helping. Or maybe you are throwing your hands up in frustration. Before we go on to the several ways parents can really help, take a few minutes to look over this quiz. See how many ring true:

1. I can't help screaming at my son—he deserves it.
2. I'm always reassuring my daughter, calming her fears by saying, "Don't be silly."
3. Criticize? How can I not when I see his bad grades!
4. It's impossible to get my daughter to talk to me—no matter what I do.
5. I can't help but feel something's wrong with my son. But since everything seems fine at home and at school, I guess it's all in my mind.
6. My daughter's really been tearing into me lately, and I don't know what to do about it.
7. I try to discuss things calmly with my son, but we always end up in a fight.
8. My daughter wears too much makeup—and when I start to tell her to wash it off because she looks cheap, she gets mad at me.
9. Therapy? My son doesn't need therapy. He needs discipline, that's all!
10. My daughter's been talking about death, and I've been telling her to stop it. She's being ridiculous!
11. My son seems depressed, but it's not a problem. He tells me it's because school is such a drag.
12. When my daughter complained about her weight, I suggested she go on a healthy diet. She lost weight—but she's still depressed.
13. When we moved, I did everything I could to make my kids feel better. I kept telling them that everything was wonderful and that we were all going to be fine. I almost believed it myself!
14. Why shouldn't I tell my son when he's wrong? That's what parents are for!
15. When I asked my daughter about her moping around the house, she told me that she was just overworked. As soon as she got out of Ms. Bresley's class, she'd be fine. "Don't be worried," she said. I'm not.

If you've agreed with any of these statements, you could be helping your depressed teen in better ways. Here's how:

THE SEVEN BEST WAYS PARENTS CAN HELP THEIR DEPRESSED TEENS

1. *"I'm Not Nagging, I'm Just Explaining!*

Jeffrey was a well-balanced teen—until Gloria, his girlfriend, broke up with him for another guy on the basketball team. He was crushed, and his depression started to build. For over two weeks, he stopped cleaning his room. He played his stereo behind closed doors all night long. In the morning, he would fight with his mother, picking up his books and storming out of the house. At night, he would fight with his father, slamming down his fork and leaving his dinner untouched. But when asked, Jeffrey blamed his problems on Gloria. She was a creep and he just had to get over her.

But Jeffrey's symptoms of depression were being masked by the breakup. It was an excuse. Underneath was a terrifying fear of rejection and a pain he just couldn't throw away.

Since Jeffrey didn't understand himself, how could his parents? To them, he was being a pain in the neck—sloppy, rude and crazy. It was natural that they'd start complaining about him, instead of seeing that beneath his obnoxious behavior was a teen in trouble.

The Parent Trap: Criticism that only clouds the issue and that can be avoided.

2. *Of Course I'm Right!"*

Ellen's mother was driving. Ellen sat in the passenger seat, watching the road and thinking about the dress her mother had promised to buy her at the mall. They took the exit to the shopping center and found a toll booth with no guard—only an automatic machine. The toll was ten cents. Ellen's mother didn't have any more change. Neither did Ellen. Saying, "Forget about it. This is silly," Ellen's mother went past the machine and kept driving. Ellen was horrified. "Mom. You just went through a toll. That's illegal. You always told me to obey the law. You're a criminal!"

When children are small, their entire world is their parents. Since they are completely dependent on their mothers and fathers, they will overvalue them in order to feel safe, turning them into all-powerful, all-knowing gods. In fact, a study of children during World War II's Battle of Britain found that if parents weren't overly anxious, their youngsters wouldn't be afraid. They would show no fear when they heard the bombs or the air raid shelter sirens. But when the parents were extremely scared themselves, their kids were, too. They felt that their world was literally crumbling around them. . . .

Enter the teenage years. Teens are expected to start taking care of themselves. Looking at their mothers and fathers as gods, all-powerful and always right, will not do great things for their self-image. We all might feel we have Superman for a father when we're young, but it's awfully hard to go out in the world and prove our independence if we continue to believe it as adults.

So . . . teens will have to stomp on their parents' pedestals to bring them down to earth. They have to see them crumble so that they can have an easier time pulling away and becoming independent.

There's also a process, called the "straw men" situation by Erik Erikson, that comes into play. When young children see their parents as all-powerful, they also see their parent's prohibitions and expectations as all-encompassing—and terrifying when crossed. When you're young, there's nothing worse than a parent finding out that you've sneaked into the cookie jar, or that you spilled ink all over the carpet.

If kids were to carry this terrible "conscience" around all their lives, they would spend their adult years being scared to death. It must be destroyed. Here's how:

At the same time teens are starting to destroy their parents' pedestals, they will also be unconsciously setting their parents up to make them believe the worst. A daughter might wear promiscuous clothes so her parents will think she's hanging out with the wrong types. A son might act like he's not doing his homework so his parents will think he's not performing well in school. Their parents, understandably upset, will start criticizing and complaining. Their sons and daughters can now take that scary internal conscience and put it "outside" onto their parents, making them "straw men." The teens will say, "I can't believe you're accusing me of that! You're not perfect either! I'm innocent." Thus, they can punish their "straw men" parents instead of themselves—and have the added plus of simultaneously toppling their parents' pedestals. Like killing two birds with one stone, bringing parents down to earth and destroying an infantile conscience are both done with the same outburst.

But outbursts can bring pain. It's important for parents to remember that even as their teens look at them with this new, critical eye, they still value them above all other role models. Even though they complain that you "broke the law" or that you "don't know anything," your teens are growing and developing—and still care very, very much.

Teens need to be unkind to their parents in order to grow—and they don't stop to realize that they might also be hurting you in the process. Let's face it: To be toppled is not fun. To know your teen no longer idolizes you is tough to accept. But it's necessary. Your best bet to stop the flow of unkind words is to resist your urge to show you are right—even when you unequivocably are.

The good news is that teens can't live with the fact that they have "creeps" for parents for long. Eventually, they will say, "Okay, my parents are human. They have some weaknesses, but they're good people. They tried. In fact, they're a lot like me. I'm a lot like them. I'm different, but we're on the same plane."

They mature—without your having to say "you're wrong and I'm right.

Parent Trap: Being right—and voicing it too often.

3. "Talk to Me"

Alice tried talking to her teenage daughter Jennifer. She really did. Every time Jennifer would go upstairs, close her bedroom door, and play her sorrowful music, Alice would knock and ask if anything was wrong. Jennifer would shake her head and say leave me alone. Alice would ask again. Jennifer would finally say that school was a drag. Alice would then make some suggestions and say some words of comfort. "I remember how much I hated school, too. But we all have to go..." She took what Jennifer said at face value.

Whether she was dialing the phone, making dinner, or leaving the house to go to work, Alice always took a few minutes out to ask her daughter if she was okay. But Jennifer never responded with anything other than school—and she wasn't getting any better.

On the surface, it looked like mother and daughter talked a lot, but in actuality they never did. Communication is an art that can only be productive with "quality time." When Jennifer started complaining about school, Alice could have pushed even further: "Okay, I can understand that school's a drag, but tell me more. How does it make you feel? It seems to me that it's affecting other areas of your life, Jennifer. You're not seeing your friends anymore. You're sitting up here in your room every weekend..."

If you show teens that you really want to talk about what's going on, you will find, more times than not, a lurking depression beneath their excuses. They might start to cry or grow sad—or even slip out the fact that they don't know whether life is worth it.

It might be hard to get teens to open up, but it is *almost always possible*—if you make it clear you really want to listen. And it can save tragedy from striking.

Parent Trap: A lack of communication that fosters depression.

FALSE FACES

MYTH: By the time teens reach adulthood, their identities are in place.

FACT: Though Erik Erikson showed that finding one's identity is the most crucial task of adolescence, it does not stop there. Nor should it. Almost every adult, at one time or another, has asked him or herself, "Who am I? Why am I doing what I'm doing? Where am I going?" The questions always remain the same. It's the answers that change over time.

---

4. "I Can't Put My Finger on It, But Something's Wrong . . ."

Every time his dad looked worried, Billy would tell him not to bother. "It's just because of English Lit. Mr. Kay's a moron. As soon as I'm out of there, everything will be super." His dad still didn't feel right, but Billy's schoolwork was up to par, his friends were still hanging around every weekend, and his game on the football field was getting him more dates than ever. Maybe he was only imagining things. . . .

But when school let out for the summer and English Lit. was only a memory, Billy still moped around the house. Instead of lifting, his depression got worse.

Trust your hunches and your instincts. You know your child. You've been living with him or her a long time. If you sense that something's different or wrong, it's important to persist—even intrude, if necessary—to get to the root of the problem. Don't be put off by English Lit. explanations or fights with friends. Show interest, express concern, and be there. Depression doesn't go away by ignoring it.

Parent Trap: Discounting your intuition that trouble lies below the surface.

5. "You Don't Really Mean That."

Every time Sonia said she felt miserable, that no one liked her and she'd never go out on a date, her mother would say, "Oh, don't be silly. You don't really mean that. You'll feel better after a good night's sleep." Whatever it was—school, friends, or a move to another town—her mother would always echo these words.

But teens are people, too, and they have a right to their feelings. We owe it to our teens to take what they say and feel seriously, and to tell them that we are concerned and sense a need for help. Ignoring their feelings will make them feel worse—and more alone.

Parent Trap: Not validating your teen's emotions.

6. "I Could Use a Good Laugh."

I often say to parents, "Adolescents need to remove us from

the pedestals we were placed on when they were young children, and see us for what we are—with the holes in our socks." During one of my lecture tours, I remember a parent standing up and exclaiming, "It's okay if they see the holes in my socks, but do they have to steal my shoes!" Another time, a different parent jumped up and said, "I feel like I'm walking around barefoot!"

Humor is great medicine. It helped Norman Cousins recover from what was supposedly a fatal illness. It helped Patricia Neal make a startling comeback from a stroke. It helped countless more get over the dark times in life. And, as parents, it can help us cope better with our teen's changeable moods and impossible behavior.

Humor also shows us that we are not alone. From Erma Bombeck and Bill Cosby to our next door neighbors, every parent has gone through the same frustrations and pain as you at some point—and the ones who survive best have learned to laugh through those years.

Parent Trap: Taking the trials and tribulations of raising a teen too seriously—and making your frustrations an even heavier burden.

7. "A Person's Gotta Do What a Person's Gotta Do."

Craig was a depressed teen who had had some skirmishes with the law. His school grades had dropped, and he had difficulty keeping friends. He lashed out at home, from yelling at his parents to throwing things around the room. Craig needed help, and had started individual therapy with me. When I approached his family about their participation, they shook their heads. No one they knew was in therapy. Besides, it was Craig's problem. Why did they have to be involved. He'd caused enough pain already!

But if Craig was suffering from a kidney disorder, they'd go to the clinic and learn about dialysis. If he'd broken his leg, the family would have gathered around to make his convalescence more comfortable.

Depression, too, deserves a family's full attention.

Adolescent depression is a family problem—I can't emphasize this enough. In order to really help your teen, you must be open to therapy yourself. Families need and deserve help.

- To deal with the demands and pressures a depressed teen creates.
- To sort out what responses help—and which hurt.
- To see that they might be withdrawing from the depressed teen and re-forming a family group that excludes him or her. This is especially true in families where other siblings are going through life with little turmoil. It's easy to concentrate on the healthier brothers and sisters, which will only isolate the depressed teen even more.

Family therapy will help families deal with these problems, and keep them actively and beneficially involved with their troubled teen, even as the depression lifts.

Parent Trap: A prejudice against therapy for their teen and for themselves.

Seven practical suggestions. Seven ways to help your teenager through depression. Alone, they might not be enough. But combined with the insights and the treatments you've read about earlier, they can go far indeed.

Adolescent depression is not a curse—on your teen or yourself. It is an illness that can be cured . . . with your help.

But general advice is one thing. Concrete, real-life situations are another. Let's go on to the common questions parents have asked me over the years now.

CHAPTER TEN

Common Questions Parents Ask

"Last night, my daughter surprised me with a hug. 'I love you, Mom. You're great!' she said. I guess that's what makes all the other stuff worthwhile."

—Parent of a 16-year-old

Every teenager—and every problem situation—is unique. But in my twenty-five years as an adolescent psychiatrist and lecturer to various parent groups across the country, I've seen the same questions crop up again and again.

Here then are some of these questions—and the answers I've given troubled parents about their troubled teens. I hope they help.

1. *My teenage son stays in his room with the door closed from the moment he comes home from school. How can I get him to talk to me?*

Remember, it is *almost always possible* to get your teen to talk if you are persistent enough. But persistence doesn't mean banging on the bedroom door and running in like a prize-winning quarterback. Persistence means a delicate balance between allowing your teen room to feel what he's feeling and intruding just enough so he knows you're there—and that you care. Whether it's getting tickets to a ballgame, planning a family trip, or making a dinner with all his favorite foods, these "pushes" translate into "I'm here. I'm ready to listen. I support you."

But don't get hostile if your gestures aren't appreciated at first. Just because you spent half the day tracking down box seats doesn't mean your son must be beholden to you. He's already feeling enough pressure!

Give him time. When he shows the slightest hint that he wants to talk—from hanging around the kitchen to driving with just you in the car—bring up his problems. But do it gently. Be calm. And if he just doesn't communicate, despite your best intentions, a trip to a counselor might be advisable.

2. *I realize my son needs help. But he refuses to see a therapist. How do I get him into therapy when he just doesn't want to go?*

For many parents, the problem lies not in whether or not the therapeutic process is working, but in getting their depressed child to go see a counselor in the first place. In my book *The Fragile Alliance,* I describe a dialogue between a father whose troubled 15-year-old son refused to go for counseling and a therapist:

> FATHER: I don't think he'll come. He's already mad at us, especially my wife. He'll think we're trying to say that he's crazy.
> THERAPIST: Do you think that he is?
> FATHER: No, but he is acting very strangely.
> THERAPIST: I wonder if he's afraid that he may be going crazy. Maybe you should discuss your concern with him. Tell him that you are worried about him and that you think he is probably worried about himself.
> FATHER: What if he still doesn't want to come, even after all that?
> THERAPIST: From what you tell me, that's very likely the way it will be. What do you feel you should do as his father if it turns out that way?
> FATHER: (*After a long pause*) He'll be there.

There is no way around your child's pain. That first visit must be made—with or without your teen's cooperation. Your son might cry or curse the whole way there in the car, but he'll go.

He simply has no other choice—once you sincerely decide that there *is* no other reasonable option.

3. *My daughter has always done great in school. But lately all she can do is talk about boys—and her schoolwork has dropped. What can I do?*

Although this might sound hard to do—nothing. At least not at first. As we have seen, adolescents go through many transitions—including their sexuality. Ask any teenager and you'll find that attracting the opposite sex is of paramount concern. But, contrary to popular opinion, teenagers are *not* jumping into intimate liaisons with each other. A study done of teenaged boys and girls found that only 37 percent of girls and 53 percent of boys have had sexual relationships by the time they were seventeen. For teenagers living at home with both parents, the percentages are even lower. Kids still look up to their parents more than any other role models—even if they act as if they don't. They look to their parents for support and they internalize their values early on. Add to this the fact that most kids are too busy trying to keep up with the world of school, grades, competition, and fitting in. Although they may be more active sexually than we were, they simply don't have the time or the inclination to be promiscuous.

Teens are more sensible—and aware—than you think. They don't want to practice a behavior that can have dire social consequences, especially in today's world. Eventually, your daughter's grades should start building up again, it's in her own best interest. In the meantime, you might want to talk to her in a logical manner and suggest that if her grades were better, she would do better in the outside world. You may have to set some limits on the social preoccupation and continue to expect time devoted to homework. But, above all, relax. Your daughter's changing sexuality will find a steadier course. If, after several months, her grades continue to drop and her behavior hasn't changed, you might want to talk to a school counselor or an outside therapist. If there is actually a major problem, your daughter is likely to call it to your attention with flagrant behavior designed to show you that she feels out of control.

4. *How can I get my son to stop hanging around with the "wrong crowd"?*

Saying "no" won't work. It will probably get him to hang out with them even more—just to defy you. All teens go through many groups of friends as they grow up, searching and hoping for that security they need as they leave dependency in their parents behind. But you can speed up the process.

I remember a mother who didn't like the boys her son was hanging around with. Instead of demanding he stop seeing them, she took a different tack. She invited them all for dinner. During the meal, the boys were as bad as she had imagined: They were impolite, crude, and rude to her. Her son was embarrassed. By seeing his friends in his home environment, the boy saw that they weren't as terrific as he had thought. He didn't tell his mother she was right (after all, that would have given her too much power), but he did drop his so-called friends.

On the other hand, if you try to find out what your teen's "wrong crowd" is really like, you just might be pleasantly surprised. They might not be as bad as you had thought. But whether good, bad, or ugly, you must have confidence in your child and the values you have instilled in him. Chances are, he'll come around.

However, if being with the "wrong crowd" leads your youngster to break family rules, consequences must follow. These consequences may include losing contact with friends for a short time. It's not your child's friends that matter, it's how he behaves with them.

5. *I think my son is doing drugs. How can I be sure—and how can I get him to stop?*

If your son exhibits any of the symptoms I discussed in Chapter Five—from withdrawal and red eyes to unpredictable behavior—you not only have a right to intrude . . . you must. His life could be at stake. Remember, too, that this is an exception to the "wrong crowd" advice. Changing "friends" to a drug-involved group may be an early sign of serious drug involvement.

If you find any evidence of drugs in his room or around the house, *don't deny their existence* by shoving your fears under the rug. And don't confront him. It will just make him defensive and annoyed at you for invading his privacy.

You can try to explain the problems that can occur with drugs, but chances are it won't work. Unfortunately, most kids won't believe the worst: "That might be true for other guys, but not me."

You can also show him that you support him, that you care about his feelings, so that he might find healthier ways to cope with teenage life.

And by all means contact medical help before it is too late. Effective treatment involves getting help *sooner* than later. Find out about any drug treatment programs in your community. (If there is none, call 1-800-COCAINE, a 24-hour national helpline.) If your son's problems don't seem severe, help on an outpatient basis might be all he needs—and medical insurance usually covers it if the program is part of a clinic or hospital unit. But if your son exhibits severe symptoms, the answer is hospitalization. Check the appendix for the names of those hospitals where teenagers on drugs have been treated successfully.

FAMOUS FACES

The Jarretts were *Ordinary People*. If their eldest son hadn't drowned in a boating accident, everything might have gone on just fine. But now their younger son is an only child, who's been back from the hospital one month. He, too, had been on that boat when his brother died. Ridden with guilt and sorrow, he had tried to commit suicide.

Now, at home, nobody's talking about the accident, about the attempted suicide—or to each other. The boy's mother refuses to acknowledge that anything is wrong with her son. His father tries to help both mother and son—and is accused of not taking sides. One son might have tragically died, but now there are four victims . . . This study of ordinary people faced with tragedy was both a best-selling book by Judith Guest and a successful movie directed by Robert Redford. It starred Mary Tyler Moore as the mother, Donald Sutherland as the father, and Timothy Hutton as their troubled son.

6. *My daughter's good friend had a fatal accident. What can I do to help her through this crisis?*

When suicide strikes, the entire community gets involved. It should be the same with a tragic accidental death. Communication is crucial to be sure that your daughter—and her friends—go through a normal grief reaction. Guilt, anger, excessive sadness—all are normal unless they last too long. If any of these symptoms turn into a long-term depression, with its characteristic weight loss or gain, withdrawal, anxiety, and irrational behavior, be sure to have her seek professional help. In the meantime, discussion at home and in the classroom about the tragedy, about the girl who got killed, about the meaning of life and death, can help. A teenager's death should not be swept under the carpet; teens, too, should be aware that life is not always pleasant, that it is not always happy—as much as we all wish it were.

7. *My son has just been diagnosed as having ADHD (Attention-Deficit Hyperactivity Disorder). What should I do?*

As we have seen in Chapter Six, ADHD is a frustrating illness, but one that can be controlled. Since your child probably does better in one-on-one situations, you might check out a different school where:

- Small classes give each child more individual attention
- Course structure is designed to stimulate teens so they won't be bored
- Lots of physical activity helps release that excess energy.

If you decide to keep your teen in the school he's currently attending, work with the guidance counselor. Seek out professional medical help. Schools as well as local hospitals should have listings of community groups, tutorial programs, and therapists who can help with this disorder.

In some cases medication may be helpful but is most useful as part of an overall treatment plan.

8. *My daughter keeps screaming, "You don't understand me!" What can I do—short of telling her to shut up!*

Your daughter might be acting insolent, but she's hurting too. It's very possible that her screams are really hiding a plea: "I'm scared to death! I'm so confused by life! You're my mother— why can't you make it better for me?"

Listen to this story from *The Fragile Alliance*, told to me by one of my young patients:

> A teenage boy approached his father with questions about the conflict in Nicaragua, abortion, the government's role in social programs, and the like. He wanted his father to give him clear-cut judgments and answers, but instead the father, after each question, equivocated, noting that the situation was very complex and that there was no simple answer. He ended his comments each time by saying "You're just going to have to make up your own mind on that, son." After this happened five times, the son finally said, "Dad, would you rather I wouldn't bother you with all these questions?" "Gosh no!" said the father. "You have to ask questions. How else are you going to learn?"

Maybe you too aren't really listening to your daughter. As this young patient learned, it can be terrifying to realize that your parents don't have all the answers . . . but it is part of growing up.

The next time your daughter says, "You don't understand me!" quietly and calmly ask her *why* she feels that way—instead of countering with "I understand you better than you think!" in the same high-pitched tone. The answer might surprise you and give you clues as to what she wants . . . and how she needs to be reassured.

9. *My son is always working hard at school—always pushing, always getting nervous before an exam, always on the go. Some parents would call this admirable, but it makes me nervous. It doesn't seem normal. Is it?*

You seem to be describing a Type A teen, the overachiever I've talked about throughout this book. I would suggest that you get him into therapy so he can discuss his feelings of inadequacy, feelings that are making him strive to be perfect in order to get approval and love. In the meantime, support him. Tell him that you love him—and why—in ways that have nothing to do with his As or his Student Council presidency. Firmly and consistently show that love and work with his therapist.

10. *My daughter had a fight with her best friend. She's absolutely miserable. What can I do to ease her pain?*

This is another hard one—because the answer, once again, is nothing. Learning to deal with rejection and pain is part of growing up. Only then can your daughter understand her values—and realize that her best friend was probably not the best person for her to be friendly with in the first place. Perhaps your daughter was only drawn to the girl because she was a part of the "right crowd." Perhaps she saw the girl as the epitome of cool—everything your daughter felt that she herself was not. Whatever it was, your daughter will eventually learn to be friendly with kids who share her values, who enjoy the same things—and who won't arbitrarily hurt her.

In the meantime, the best thing to do is listen. Discuss your daughter's feelings with her, and let her see the anger beneath her tears. Help her express that anger. Let her see that there were things she didn't like about her best friend. Share some stories from your own past. You survived. So will she. But if your daughter's depression does not lift after a few weeks, I would advise professional counseling.

11. *We've recently discovered that our son has a learning disability. What are the resources available to him?*

In today's world, learning disabilities are being discovered earlier and earlier, stopping a teen's depression and pain before it takes root. For less severe cases, there is remedial reading or math tutoring, special classes. For more severely handicapped teens, there are specialized schools throughout the country that are designed to help the learning disabled. There are also community-based self-help groups to help parents cope. Check with your local hospital or school for a complete listing of available resources.

To paraphrase an old saying: Help will be there when you're ready to accept it. Be ready. Be open. Observe. And above all, listen—to your teen and to yourself.

EPILOGUE

The Face of Hope

"Yeah, there's still a lot I don't understand. But that's okay. It's really okay. Life is good."

—*Former teenage drug addict.*

George Bernard Shaw once said that youth was wasted on the young. But I don't believe that's so. If our young knew and understood what we as adults know, they'd never take risks. They'd never try—and they'd never show us their fresher, newer outlook on life.

Someone I know who'd recently gone through a crisis told me that she'd handled it because she had to. Perhaps it's the same with our kids. The young need their naiveté just as adults need their wisdom to survive.

I remember the mother of a teen who'd come to see me. Her son was making great improvement, and she was pleased. "What's your magic, Dr. Meeks? Why are you able to do what I have tried for years to do without success?"

I shook my head. Yes, I have years of experience in dealing with adolescent problems. Yes, I understand the treatment process and the inroads made in medicine and technology. But, most importantly, I listen—and communicate. And often I'm not really sure what the adolescents found in our talks to heal themselves.

We have a lot we can learn from our teens—and vice versa. But we need to talk. Throughout this book, I've emphasized that adolescent depression is a family problem. And it is. Families must go to therapy as much as their teens. Communication must open up. It's the best inoculation against depression. A family whose members communicate with one another and who listen and respect one another's feelings can do more than any one doctor, any one school, and any one theory.

We have now seen how teens are really different than adults, with minds and bodies that are going through a vast sea of changes. We have seen how depression can strike—and why. And we have seen how drugs, learning disabilities, conduct disorders, and suicides all add their price. But we have also seen the vast array of treatments that are available today.

Thanks to the technology, research, and resources available to doctors today, we can do much to help our depressed youth.

But the cold, hard fact remains that some teens go through life perfectly fine—and others are riddled with turmoil. In some cases, it's easy to point the finger. Family history, lifestyle, chemical imbalance—any of these could be valid reasons. But not always. As we have seen, the best parents can sometimes have troubled teens. It's the luck of the draw.

There's no need to blame yourself. You have done the best that you could. And if you must seek outside help, that, too, is doing the best for your child.

Depression is treatable. The response is good and the outlook is positive. Your depressed teen has youth on his or her side. She or he is resilient—and able to bounce back better than their world-weary parents.

The answer I gave that happy mother when she approached me about her recovered son was: "It doesn't really matter, does it? The fact is that your child is getting better—and that's what counts."

Do what counts. With the proper help—and support—from you, the prognosis for a cure is excellent.

Your teen is not alone. Neither are you.

Your teen's future is waiting. And so is yours.

Godspeed.

Sources

Alsop, Peter, Ph.D. "How do you Eat an Elephant?? One Bite at a Time!" *Report of the National Conference on Youth Suicide*, National Conference on Youth Suicide, June 19-20, 1985, Washington, D.C. Co-Sponsored by the Department of Health and Human Services, Administration for Children, Youth, and Families, and the Youth Suicide National Center.

American Psychiatric Association, *The Diagnostic and Statistical Manual of Mental Disorders*, 3rd edition revised. Washington DC: American Psychiatric Association, 1987.

Associated Press, "Advice is Offered on Mass Suicide," *The Boston Globe*, August 26, 1988.

Berendzen, Richard, Ph.D. "Surviving College: Teaching College Students to Cope," *Report of the National Conference on Youth Suicide*, National Conference on Youth Suicide, June 19-20, 1985, Washington, D.C. Co-Sponsored by the Department of Health and Human Services, Administration for Children, Youth, and Families, and the Youth Suicide National Center.

Berland, Jeffrey L., Extein, Irl, and Kirstein, Larry S. *Guide to the New Medicines of the Mind*, Summit, NJ: The PIA Press, 1988.

Bolton, Iris M. "Survival: Strategies for Healing," *Report of the National Conference on Youth Suicide*, National Conference on Youth Suicide, June 19-20, 1985, Washington, D.C. Co-Sponsored by the Department of Health and Human Services, Administration for Children, Youth, and Families, and the Youth Suicide National Center.

Byrne, Robert, *The Other 637 Best Things Anybody Ever Said*, New York: Fawcett Crest, 1984.

Byrne, Robert, *The Third—And Possibly the Best—637 Best Things Anybody Ever Said*, New York: Atheneum, 1986.

Cadwalader, George, *Castaways: The Penikese Island Experiment*, Chelsea, VT: Chelsea Green Publishing Company, 1988.

Chatlos, Calvin, with Lawrence D. Chilnick. *Crack: What You Should Know About the Cocaine Epidemic*, New York: Perigee Books. 1987.

Frazier, Shervert H., "Preventing Youth Suicide: A Collaborative Effort," *Report of the National Conference on Youth Suicide*, National Conference on Youth Suicide, June 19-20, 1985, Washington, D.C. Co-Sponsored by the Department of Health and Human Services, Administration for Children, Youth, and Families, and the Youth Suicide National Center.

Gold, Mark S. *The Good News About Depression*. New York: Villard Books. 1987.

Grossman, Laurie M. "Atomic War Among Top Fears of U.S. and Soviet Teen-Agers," *The Washington Post*, August 18, 1988.

Hansen, William B., Malotte, C. Kevin, and Fielding, Jonathan E. "Tobacco and Alcohol Prevention: Preliminary Results of a Four-Year Study," *Adolescent Psychiatry: Developmental and Clinical Studies, Annals of the American Society for Adolescent Psychiatry*, Volume 14, Edited by Sherman C. Feinstein, Editor-in-Chief; Aaron H. Esman, John G. Looney, George H. Orvin, John L. Schimel, Allan Z. Schwartzberg, Arthur D. Sorosky, Max Sugar, Senior Editors, The University of Chicago Press, Chicago and London, 1987.

Hardy, Dorcas R. "Introductory Statement," *Report of the National Conference on Youth Suicide*, National Conference on Youth Suicide, June 19-20, 1985, Washington, D.C. Co-Sponsored by the Department of Health and Human Services, Administration for Children, Youth, and Families, and the Youth Suicide National Center.

Hardy, Molly, "Students Against Suicide," *Report of the National Conference on Youth Suicide*, National Conference on Youth Suicide, June 19-20, 1985, Washington, D.C. Co-Sponsored by the Department of Health and Human Services, Administration for Children, Youth, and Families, and the Youth Suicide National Center.

Hertzman, Marc, "Alcohol, Drugs and Adolescent Suicide," *Report of the National Conference on Youth Suicide*, National Conference on Youth Suicide, June 19-20, 1985, Washington, D.C. Co-Sponsored by the Department of Health and Human Services, Administration for Children, Youth, and Families, and the Youth Suicide National Center.

Jennings, Kay Donahue, Ph.D. Connors, Robin E. Ph.D. and Stegman, Charles E. Ph.D. "Does a Physical Handicap Alter the Development of Mastery Motivation During the Preschool Years?" *Journal of the American Academy of Child and Adolescent Psychiatry*, Volume 27, Number 3, May 1988.

Kahn, Aman U. "Biochemical Profile of Depressed Adolescents," *Journal of the American Academy of Child Psychiatry*, volume 26, pages 873–878, 1987.

Kett, Joseph F. *Rites of Passage: Adolescence in America 1790 to the Present*, New York: Basic Books, 1977.

Lettieri, Dan J. Ph.D. "Clues to Adolescent Suicide," *Report of the National Conference on Youth Suicide*, National Conference on Youth Suicide, June 19-20, 1985, Washington, D.C. Co-Sponsored by the Department of Health and Human Services, Administration for Children, Youth, and Families, and the Youth Suicide National Center.

Levine, Saul V. "The Myths and Needs of Contemporary Youth," *Adolescent Psychiatry: Developmental and Clinical Studies, Annals of the American Society for Adolescent Psychiatry,* Volume 14, Edited by Sherman C. Feinstein, Editor-in-Chief; Aaron H. Esman, John G. Looney, George H. Orvin, John L. Schimel, Allan Z. Schwartzberg, Arthur D. Sorosky, Max Sugar, Senior Editors. Chicago and London: The University of Chicago Press. 1987.

Lipton, Terry David, and Leader, Elaine. "Teen Line—A Mental Health Delivery System for Youth," *Report of the National Conference on Youth Suicide,* National Conference on Youth Suicide, June 19-20, 1985, Washington, D.C. Co-Sponsored by the Department of Health and Human Services, Administration for Children, Youth, and Families, and the Youth Suicide National Center.

Litowitz, Bonnie E. and Gundlach, Robert A. "When Adolescents Write: Semiotic and Social Dimensions of Adolescents' Personal Writing," *Adolescent Psychiatry: Developmental and Clinical Studies, Annals of the American Society for Adolescent Psychiatry,* Volume 14, Edited by Sherman C. Feinstein, Editor-in-Chief; Aaron H. Esman, John G. Looney, George H. Orvin, John L. Schimel, Allan Z. Schwartzberg, Arthur D. Sorosky, Max Sugar, Senior Editors. Chicago and London: The University of Chicago Press. 1987.

Livingston, Dodie Truman, "Foreword," *Report of the National Conference on Youth Suicide,* National Conference on Youth Suicide, June 19-20, 1985, Washington, D.C. Co-Sponsored by the Department of Health and Human Services, Administration for Children, Youth, and Families, and the Youth Suicide National Center.

McGee, Rob, Ph.D. and Share, David L. "Attention Deficit Disorder-Hyperactivity and Academic Failure: Which Comes First and What Should be Treated?" *Journal of the American Academy of Child and Adolescent Psychiatry,* Volume 27, Number 3, May 1988.

Meeks, John E. "Treatment of the Suicidal Adolescent," *Report of the National Conference on Youth Suicide*, National Conference on Youth Suicide, June 19-20, 1985, Washington, D.C. Co-Sponsored by the Department of Health and Human Services, Administration for Children, Youth, and Families, and the Youth Suicide National Center.

Meeks, John E. "Adolescent Substance Abuse: Etiology and Dynamics," *Basic Handbook of Child Psychiatry*, Volume 5, 388–393, 1987.

Meeks, John E. "Diagnosis and Treatment of Common Adolescent Depressive States," 1987.

Meeks, John E. "Evaluation and Management of Suicidal Risk in Chemically Dependent Adolescents," 1986.

Meeks, John E. *The Fragile Alliance: An Orientation to the Psychiatric Treatment of the Adolescent*, 3rd edition. Malabar, FL: Robert E. Krieger Publishing Co., 1986.

Meeks, John E. *The Many Faces of Adolescent Depression*, The Psychiatric Institute of Montgomery County, Rockville, MD., 1987.

Mitchell, Lonnie E. Ph.D. "The Effect of Drug Abuse on Suicide Rates Among Black Youth in the District of Columbia," *Report of the National Conference on Youth Suicide*, National Conference on Youth Suicide, June 19-20, 1985, Washington, D.C. Co-Sponsored by the Department of Health and Human Services, Administration for Children, Youth, and Families, and the Youth Suicide National Center.

Motto, Jerome A. "Clinical and Empirical Criteria for Estimation of Suicide Risk in Adolescents," *Report of the National Conference on Youth Suicide*, National Conference on Youth Suicide, June 19-20, 1985, Washington, D.C. Co-Sponsored by the Department of Health and Human Services, Administration for Children, Youth, and Families, and the Youth Suicide National Center.

Offer, Daniel, "The Mystery of Adolescence," *Adolescent Psy-*

chiatry: Developmental and Clinical Studies, Annals of the American Society for Adolescent Psychiatry, Volume 14, Edited by Sherman C. Feinstein, Editor-in-Chief; Aaron H. Esman, John G. Looney, George H. Orvin, John L. Schimel, Allan Z. Schwartzberg, Arthur D. Sorosky, Max Sugar, Senior Editors, The University of Chicago Press, Chicago and London, 1987.

Pearson, Glen T. "Long-Term Treatment Needs of Hospitalized Adolescents," *Adolescent Psychiatry: Developmental and Clinical Studies, Annals of the American Society for Adolescent Psychiatry,* Volume 14, Edited by Sherman C. Feinstein, Editor-in-Chief; Aaron H. Esman, John G. Looney, George H. Orvin, John L. Schimel, Allan Z. Schwartzberg, Arthur D. Sorosky, Max Sugar, Senior Editors, The University of Chicago Press, Chicago and London 1987.

Peck, Michael L. and Berkovitz, Irving H. "Youth Suicide: The Role of School Consultation," *Adolescent Psychiatry: Developmental and Clinical Studies, Annals of the American Society for Adolescent Psychiatry,* Volume 14, Edited by Sherman C. Feinstein, Editor-in-Chief; Aaron H. Esman, John G. Looney, George H. Orvin, John L. Schimel, Allan Z. Schwartzberg, Arthur D. Sorosky, Max Sugar, Senior Editors, The University of Chicago Press, Chicago and London, 1987.

Peterson, Lynne F. "Dying for Attention," *Report of the National Conference on Youth Suicide,* National Conference on Youth Suicide, June 19-20, 1985, Washington, D.C. Co-Sponsored by the Department of Health and Human Services, Administration for Children, Youth, and Families, and the Youth Suicide National Center.

Rosenberg, Mark. "Suicide Clusters," *Report of the National Conference on Youth Suicide,* National Conference on Youth Suicide, June 19-20, 1985, Washington, D.C. Co-Sponsored by the Department of Health and Human Services, Administration for Children, Youth, and Families, and the Youth Suicide National Center.

Ross, Charlotte P. "Foreword," *Report of the National Conference on Youth Suicide,* National Conference on Youth Suicide, June 19-20, 1985, Washington, D.C. Co-Sponsored by the Department of Health and Human Services, Administration for Children, Youth, and Families, and the Youth Suicide National Center.

Slaby, Andrew E. *Aftershock: Overcoming Traumatic Stress in Everyday Life,* New York: Villard Books (to be published in April, 1989).

Sperling, Dan, "Today's Teens Have it Rough," *USA Today,* September 14, 1988.

Sugar, Max, "Diagnostic Aspects of Underachievement in Adolescents," *Adolescent Psychiatry: Developmental and Clinical Studies, Annals of the American Society for Adolescent Psychiatry,* Volume 14, Edited by Sherman C. Feinstein, Editor-in-Chief; Aaron H. Esman, John G. Looney, George H. Orvin, John L. Schimel, Allan Z. Schwartzberg, Arthur D. Sorosky, Max Sugar, Senior Editors, The University of Chicago Press, Chicago and London, 1987.

Velez, Carmen Noemi, and Cohen, Patricia, "Suicidal Behavior and Ideation in a Community Sample of Children: Maternal and Youth Reports," *Journal of the American Academy of Child and Adolescent Psychiatry,* Volume 27, Number 3, May 1988.

Voth, Harold M. "Social Stresses and Youth Suicide," *Report of the National Conference on Youth Suicide,* National Conference on Youth Suicide, June 19-20, 1985, Washington, D.C. Co-Sponsored by the Department of Health and Human Services, Administration for Children, Youth, and Families, and the Youth Suicide National Center.

Wilkes, T.C.R. (Chris), and Rush, A. John, "Adaptations of Cognitive Therapy for Depressed Adolescents," *Journal of the American Academy of Child and Adolescent Psychiatry,* Volume 27, Number 3, pages 381–386, May 1988.

Wyatt, Frederic T. "Teens Helping Teens," *Report of the National Conference on Youth Suicide,* National Conference on Youth Suicide, June 19-20, 1985, Washington, D.C. Co-Sponsored by the Department of Health and Human Services, Administration for Children, Youth, and Families, and the Youth Suicide National Center.

——————, "Girl Mimicking Movie Scene is Struck and Killed by Train," *The New York Times,* March 8, 1988.

——————, "Study Ties Teen-Age Suicide to Abnormalities in the Brain," *The New York Times,* May 13, 1988.

Other titles of interest...

Young, Sober & Free
by Shelly Marshall

Through intensely personal stories, young people share their experiences of living through alcoholism and other drug addiction. Their words paint a clear picture of how young people can rely on the Twelve Steps as primary recovery tools. 137 pp.
Order No. 1116

Getting a Life
The Young Person's Guide to Drug-Free Living
by Dana W., illustrated by Larry England

Issues such as sexuality, relationships, support groups, and relapse prevention techniques are explored through young people's personal stories and straightforward discussions about working a successful recovery program. 229 pp.
Order No. 5105

Feed Your Head
Some Excellent Stuff on Being Yourself
by Earl Hipp, illustrated by L. K. Hanson

Here's some fun and excellent stuff for young people to help them make their way through the daily maze of questions, worries, ups and downs, problems, and puzzles. The author and other young people provide new ideas to help young people become the people they want to be. 160 pp.
Order No. 5034

**For price and order information, or a free catalog,
please call our Telephone Representatives.**

HAZELDEN EDUCATIONAL MATERIALS

1-800-328-9000
(Toll Free. U.S., Canada,
and the Virgin Islands)

1-612-257-4010
(Outside the U.S.
and Canada)

1-612-257-1331
(24-hour FAX)

Pleasant Valley Road • P.O. Box 176 • Center City, MN 55012-0176

Hazelden Europe • P.O. Box 616 • Cork, Ireland
Phone: **Int'l Access Code+353-21-314318**
FAX: **Int'l Access Code+353-21-961269**

Index